"The fear of God is the only antido
fear of man. True fear of God does n
endears us to Him. If we want to be effective in this world as followers of Christ, we must be willing to break the power of the fear of man in our lives. In *Their Finest Hour*, R. T. Kendall once again brilliantly unpacks the truth of Scripture. Through studying the stories and decisions of those who chose to honor God above all else, we see the eternal impact made in those priceless moments. Be encouraged—this is a challenging but wonderful book. God is looking for such men and women today who will pay the price to rightly display who Jesus is to the world around them."

—**BILL JOHNSON**, senior leader, Bethel Church, Redding, California, author of *Born for Significance* and *The Way of Life*

"When an eighty-eight-year-old who has already written so many books still has something to say, I sit up and take notice. The brilliant R. T. Kendall is my oldest friend, and is also advanced in years in his teaching ministry beyond anyone else I know. However, he still carries an enduring passion for the Word of God. This devotion comes across beautifully in *Their Finest Hour*, where he identifies character traits and examples of trust, faith, and worship that were defining moments in the lives of many of God's people in Scripture. I enjoyed this reading journey so much, and I know you also will!"

—**MATT REDMAN**, songwriter and worship leader

"R. T. Kendall has an astonishing gift of expounding the Scriptures with authority, wisdom, and application to our daily lives. Everything he writes is well worth reading!"

—**NICKY GUMBEL**, retired vicar, Holy Trinity Brompton, London, England.

"The former minister of Westminster Chapel, who blessed us with *God Meant It for Good*, has produced an equally inspiring book—thirty studies on the major characters of the Bible that demonstrate in a fresh manner what true greatness is. This book is a must-read for any Christian desiring true success in life."

—**DR. ROBERT JEFFRESS,** pastor, First Baptist Church, Dallas, Bible teacher on *Pathway to Victory*

"This book is vintage Dr. R. T. Kendall. It is brimful of biblical wisdom, rich in pastoral insight, and overflowing with encouragement and challenge. Read, enjoy, and grow in truth and grace!"

—**J. JOHN,** evangelist

"I remember when this book was being written and R. T. Kendall preached 'David's Finest Hour' from our pulpit in New York City. I told R. T. that it was the best message he had ever preached—and he has preached dozens of times for Times Square Church. To now have twenty-nine more 'finest hours' in one book is a treasure. R. T. seems to capture someone's finest hour the way God would define it. I have literally read dozens of books by R. T. Kendall, and this could very well be his finest one."

—**TIM DILENA,** senior pastor, Times Square Church, author of *Your Life Is God's Story* and *The 260 Journey*

"R. T. Kendall is a treasured friend and prayer partner. I have read many of his books, and this one entitled *Their Finest Hour* may be his finest book yet."

—**DR. CHARLES REDMOND,** pastor, First Baptist Church, Pasadena, Texas

"If you need to be inspired with vision and faith in your life and leadership, then please read *Their Finest Hour.* This splendid book will be used to build leaders who will change the world. This book makes me long for all of us to experience our finest hour before we die or before the Lord Himself returns."

—**RONNIE W. FLOYD,** author, speaker, and pastor emeritus, Cross Church

"Following Jesus can be enigmatic. Sometimes it's hard to know what to do and what not to do. To be exalted, you must humble yourself. To receive, you must give. When persecuted, you must forgive. Yet such unusual mannerisms point to Christlike 'greatness.' In his new book *Their Finest Hour*, Dr. R. T. Kendall presents numerous examples of people in the Bible who manifested true greatness. Both Christ-followers and seekers will benefit from this excellent work written by a truly great man."

—**DR. STEVE GAINES,** senior pastor of Bellevue Baptist Church, Memphis, Tennessee

"This book is Dr. R. T. Kendall at his very best—it is incisive and challenging, and you get the sense that somebody has just turned on a light."

—**ROB PARSONS,** OBE, Care for the Family, United Kingdom

"The authors who have meant the most to me through the years are those who make me want to love God more when I read their works. I long to read authors who write in such a way that I need to pause and close the chapter I'm reading because I desire to spend time with the One who created me. R. T. Kendall is that kind of author, and *Their Finest Hour* is that kind of book. As you read, you will be reminded through every chapter that God works in mysterious ways and that our greatest moments in life frequently take place when we aren't thinking about ourselves at all. The latest book R. T. Kendall puts out is typically my favorite that he's written—and I now have a new favorite."

—**JARRETT STEPHENS,** senior pastor, Champion Forest Baptist Church, Houston, Texas, author of *The Always God: He Hasn't Changed and You Are Not Forgotten*

"R. T. Kendall has written another amazing book inspiring us to be faithful to God no matter what challenges we may face. I especially admire R. T.'s desire to obey and please God even if this means that some people may not be too pleased. After reading this book,

I understand that R. T.'s inspiration comes from the many examples in the Scriptures who only seek the glory from the only God (John 5:44)."

—**SAM SONG,** pastor, Solomon's Porch, Hong Kong

"R. T. Kendall wrote this book 'to encourage you to follow Jesus daily with a view to being self-effacing . . . that you might be utterly willing to go outside your comfort zone for the sole glory of God.' He suggests what 'the finest hours' of thirty very different Bible characters who chose to believe and obey the Lord were, mostly at deeply challenging times in their lives. I was so inspired by these stories—like with Habakkuk, who was so troubled at the mystery of evil but trusted God; Elijah, who agreed to put his fame in the shadows by requesting a double anointing for his successor; Sarah, who believed she'd have a baby in her old age; Ruth, who loyally stayed with her mother-in-law; and Joseph, who totally forgave the treachery of his brothers. Each of these people highlights the wonder of God's grace toward us despite our failures, personality flaws, and insignificance in worldly terms. This book could transform your walk with the Lord."

—**REV. CELIA BOWRING,** CARE

"Dr. Kendall weaves, in this tour of biblical greatness, a profound narrative of the life yielded to God. The Christian life exists upon Jesus's words 'Blessed are the poor in spirit.' Though this passage is not specifically mentioned herein, every vignette calls the reader back to poverty of spirit. Thus, when reading R. T.'s words, I have experienced a glimpse of the kingdom of God."

—**KENT REDFEARN,** pastor, Muldoon Community Assembly, Anchorage, Alaska

THEIR
FINEST HOUR

THEIR FINEST HOUR

30 Biblical Figures Who Pleased God at Great Cost

R. T. Kendall

Foreword by O. S. Hawkins

THOMAS NELSON
Since 1798

THOMAS NELSON

Their Finest Hour

Published in Nashville, Tennessee, by Thomas Nelson. Thomas Nelson is a registered trademark of HarperCollins Christian Publishing, Inc.

Thomas Nelson titles may be purchased in bulk for educational, business, fundraising, or sales promotional use. For information, please email SpecialMarkets@ThomasNelson.com.

ISBN 978-0-310-15999-5 (audio)

Library of Congress Cataloging-in-Publication Data

Names: Kendall, R. T., 1935- author.
Title: Their finest hour: 30 biblical figures who pleased God at great cost / R. T. Kendall.
Description: Nashville, Tennessee: Thomas Nelson, [2024]
Identifiers: LCCN 2023057854 (print) | LCCN 2023057855 (ebook) | ISBN 9780310159971 (softcover) | ISBN 9780310159988 (ebook)
Subjects: LCSH: Bible. Old Testament--Biography. | Bible. New Testament--Biography
Classification: LCC BS571 .K45 2024 (print) | LCC BS571 (ebook) | DDC 221.9/22--dc23/ eng/20240216
LC record available at https://lccn.loc.gov/2023057854
LC ebook record available at https://lccn.loc.gov/2023057855

Cover design: Rob Jelsema
Cover photo: Bargais / AdobeStock
Interior design: Sara Colley

Printed in the United States of America

24 25 26 27 28 LBC 5 4 3 2 1

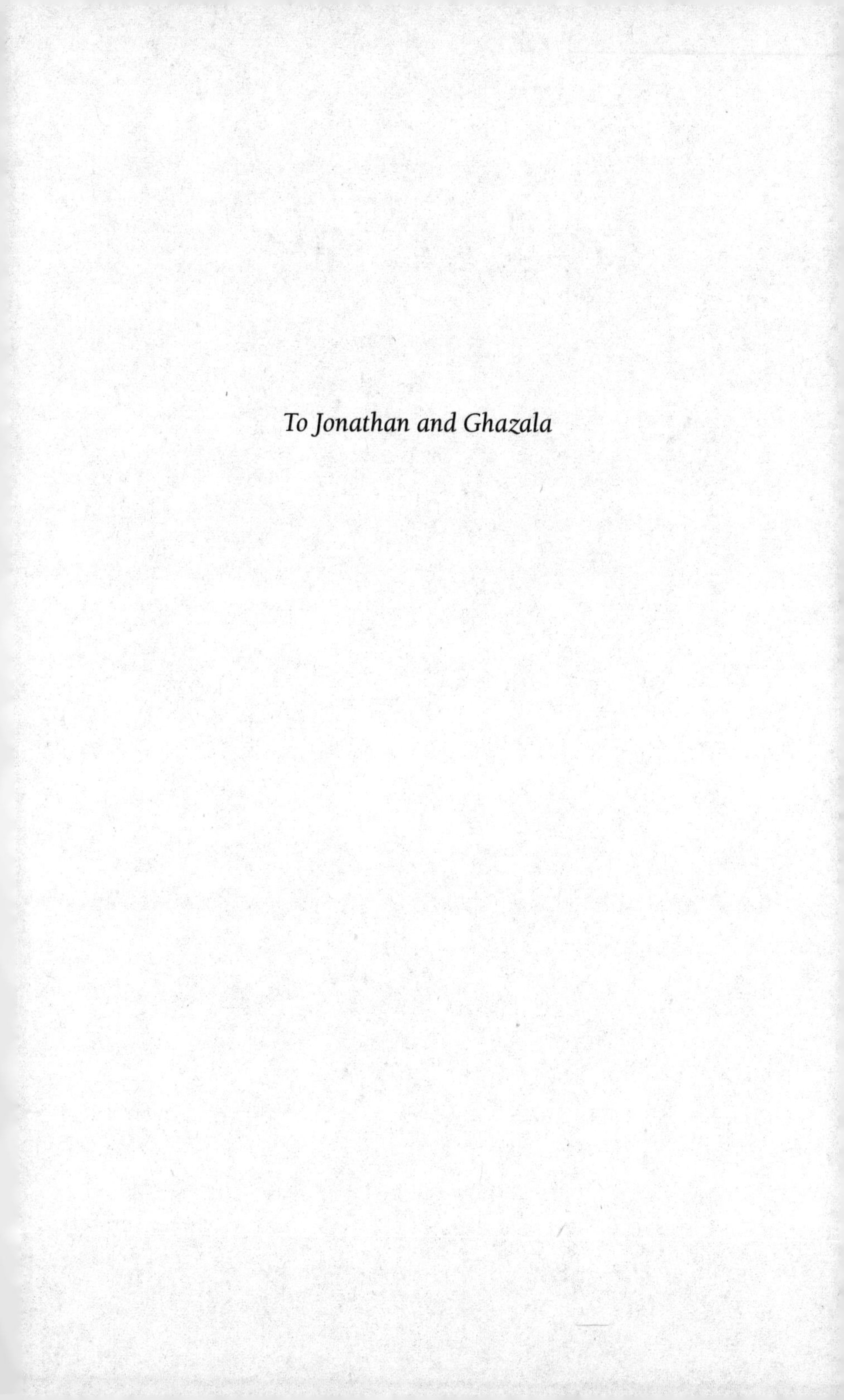

To Jonathan and Ghazala

Contents

Foreword

I have known and loved R. T. Kendall for over forty years. We exchanged pulpits every August in the 1980s when he was pastor of Westminster Chapel in London and I was pastor of First Baptist Church in Fort Lauderdale, Florida. We have talked theology for hours together in a flat bottom boat as we fished for bonefish off the coast of Bimini in the Bahamas. In many ways we have lived and loved life together for the majority of our ministry years. R. T. and Louise have been married for over sixty-four years. His reputation is spotless and his character is beyond reproach.

R. T.'s pen ranks with the most prolific of any pastor/theologian's, not simply of our lifetime but possibly over the twenty centuries of the Christian church. Many of the nearly one hundred books he has published will be considered classics for generations to come. Books like *God Meant It for God*, *Total Forgiveness*, and *Prophetic Integrity* will exist forever. It is not an exaggeration or a whim of hyperbole to say that decades after R. T. is in heaven his books, like those of Spurgeon, Bunyan, and a few others, will continue to grace the library shelves of believers.

I actually believe this volume you hold in your hand just might be R. T.'s own "finest hour" in producing a practical, thought-provoking book that I only wish I had thought of writing. As the pages unfold before you, your eyes will be opened to the "finest hours" of so many men and women whose lives and legacies have been preserved for all posterity in the greatest book ever written, the Holy Bible. And, clarified in a way that only R. T. can deliver, many of their "finest hours" came in their most challenging and defining moments.

As I read this manuscript, finished it, and laid it aside, the Holy Spirit prompted me to ask of myself, "What was my own finest hour?" I am convinced you will be prompted by Him in a similar vein, and, like me, you will be challenged to ensure that your finest hour is yet to come. You will be drawn closer to the hearts of these heroes of the faith as you journey from chapter to chapter. In this way, you will be drawn closer to the heart of God.

Thank you, my sweet friend R. T., for this lasting gift to the church of our Lord Jesus Christ.

O. S. Hawkins

Former pastor, First Baptist Church, Dallas, Texas, and author of the bestselling Code Series of devotionals, including *The Joshua Code* and *The Jesus Code*

www.oshawkins.com

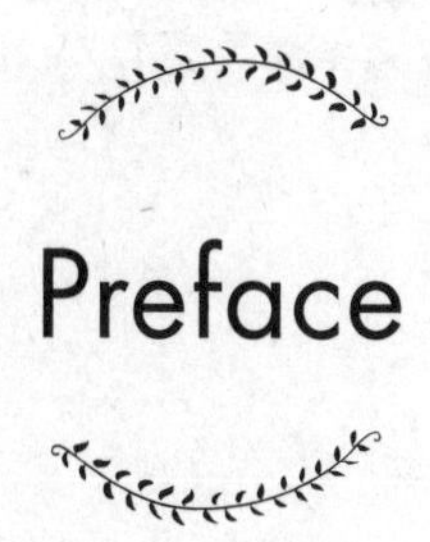

Preface

I once asked John Stott (1921–2011), "How many books have you written?" He replied, "To answer that would be like David's sin of numbering the people!"

Whereas I don't honestly know how many books I have written, I can absolutely say that Dale Williams, my acquisitions editor with HarperCollins Christian Publishing, is the kindest and most patient editor I have ever had. My debt to him in finishing this book is incalculable. That said, I continue to be most thankful to Emily Voss, my gracious marketing manager, and Daniel Saxton, the competent production editor who has the final say on what is written in this book.

My sincere and warm thanks also go to my old friend, Dr. O. S. Hawkins, for kindly writing both the foreword and afterword to this book. After a long career in both the pastorate and finance, O. S. has recently achieved the honored position of chancellor at Southwestern Baptist Theological Seminary. My deepest thanks, as always, go to my greatest friend and critic, my wife of sixty-five years, Louise.

This book is warmly dedicated to Jonathan and Ghazala David. Jonathan handled my recording and radio ministry when I was at Westminster Chapel (1977–2002). Jonathan and Ghazala remain among our closest friends in London.

Introduction

How can ye believe, which receive honour one of another, and seek not the honour that cometh from God only?
—John 5:44 KJV

All greatness is unconscious, or it is little and naught.
—Thomas Carlyle (1795–1881)

This is not a motivational book. That is, if people are looking for a formula of how to be successful, popular, or how to achieve their finest hour, this book does not provide that. And, yet, this certainly is a motivational book if one is willing to be unpopular for the honor and glory of God. Indeed, I would be humbled and gratified to no end if this book should motivate you to want to be *honored in the sight of God* but not necessarily in the eyes of people. After all, none of us will ever outgrow enjoying the praise of people. Many ancient Pharisees, for instance, missed their Messiah because they were never delivered from an addiction for approval. Jesus asked them, "How can you believe, since you accept glory from one another but don't seek the glory that comes from the only God?" (John 5:44). I cut my teeth on the Authorized King James Version, which renders the verse this way: "How can ye believe, which receive honour one of another, and seek not the honour that cometh from God only?" The KJV stresses you seek approval from God *alone*; most versions stress you seek approval from the one and only true God. Both approaches are absolutely right!

"All greatness is unconscious, or it is little and naught," said Thomas Carlyle (1795–1881). This means that if we feel we are attaining true greatness, we are probably self-deceived. We will never know until we get to heaven or shortly before, as Paul did (2 Tim. 4:8), whether we will receive God's "well done" declaration at the judgment seat of Christ (2 Cor. 5:10). I often think of a statement of Charles Spurgeon (1834–1892): "I looked to Christ and the Dove flew in; I looked at the Dove and He disappeared." These things said, I do believe that we can have an inner testimony of the Spirit that we are, in measure, pleasing God—as Enoch had received at some stage before he was translated to heaven (Heb. 11:5). In a way, this book is the application of my previous book *Pleasing God* (Thomas Nelson, 2023). After all, pleasing God is to achieve greatness in his sight but not necessarily in the sight of people.

This book is about greatness—true greatness. "Be not afraid of greatness," said Shakespeare (1564–1616) in his play *Twelfth Night*. "Some are born great, some achieve greatness, and others have greatness thrust upon them." Since greatness may be defined in more than one way, I choose to understand it in the way I believe *God* looks at it, namely, achieving greatness in *his* sight. One, therefore, can never be born with true greatness.

Neither can true greatness be thrust upon someone. Instead, true greatness must be achieved—if only for a moment. And, yet, the moment when one achieves true greatness will likely be unknown to that individual. True greatness is almost certainly an unconscious achievement.

Let me explain how I use "finest hour" in this book. What "finest hour" means to me may be different from your definition. For example, a professional tennis player might say that his or her finest hour was winning the men's or women's championship at Wimbledon, London. Possibly Aaron Judge might regard his finest hour as hitting that sixty-second home run in the 2022 baseball season, breaking the American League record. What a person did to be awarded a Nobel Prize might be seen as his or her finest hour. These things said, one could justly call my definition subjective, if not arbitrary. As "beauty is to the eye of the beholder," I see the decisions of David and Elijah and others in this book displaying a *quality of character* than which no finer—or greater—can be conceived.

Many readers will recognize the phrase "finest hour" because of the historic speech of Winston Churchill (1874–1965) in the House of Commons on June 18, 1940. With the threat of Adolf Hitler and World War II coming to grim reality across Europe, here is what he said:

> Let us therefore brace ourselves to our duties, and so bear ourselves that, if the British Empire and its Commonwealth last for a thousand years, men will still say, "This was their finest hour."

"Finest hour" is generally defined or understood as a point in time or a relatively brief period of time when an especially distinguished, admirable, or effective set of actions is performed. It usually means the moment of time of one's greatest success or achievement.

YOUR MOST SELF-EFFACING MOMENT

To experience *your* finest hour, in my view, means you achieved true greatness—at least for a moment. But in whose eyes? That is the issue. Answer: God's eyes—not what people may think. The finest hour is *your most self-effacing and God-honoring moment, when what you do is not likely going to help your reputation.*

That said, I should add: as one's tastes, needs, and interests change with age, so, too, our definition of *finest hour* may shift with time. One might have explained this phrase differently years ago. I might have chosen different events from the lives of Bible characters to demonstrate their finest hour than I would choose today—or I might have interpreted these events differently. But after being in the ministry for almost seventy years, I speak as I understand the Lord's ways today.

Another way of thinking about this issue is in terms of the debate over "character versus gifting" and which quality is more important. Some well-known church leaders hold to the idea that one's gift is more important than one's character. I disagree—I regard one's character as much more important. Therefore, when I consider biblical individuals' "finest hour" I am looking at their *character.* It is not about their intelligence—they were born with a certain IQ. It is about not the miracles they may have performed. Or their stature. Or their spiritual gifting. As I mentioned earlier, we will all stand before the judgment seat of Christ and give an account of the things done in the body "whether good or bad." If by the grace of God I should receive any reward, it will be based not on how many books I have written or how many people I have preached to, but rather this: What kind of husband, or father, was I? What kind of character did I have?

Now for the paradox of the finest hour. This moment will almost certainly be an unconscious experience. When it happens you will not say, "I am now having my finest hour." Others will more likely observe your finest hour. Or you might reflect on that moment *later*. It is unlikely that the thought of attaining to a moment of greatness entered David's mind when he would not allow the ark of the covenant to stay with him in exile. He had no idea that this was a brilliant moment. As we will see later, I doubt whether Elisha not ordering Gehazi to tell Naaman the truth about the request for money in 2 Kings 5 was a conscious self-effacing act. It is more likely that Elisha had long before become so immersed in a love for the glory of God that he would not even consider ordering Gehazi to keep Naaman from thinking Elisha accepted money. But it crossed my mind—I would have made sure Naaman knew the truth!

"DEFINING MOMENT" VERSUS "FINEST HOUR"

Allow me to clarify the difference between "defining moment" and "finest hour." A defining moment is usually when an event shapes your trajectory for life. This moment might be largely passive—something that happens to you. For instance, you could say that David's defining moment was when Samuel anointed him to be king, although he did not wear the crown of both Israel and Judah for another twenty years. Some people have more than one defining moment; David arguably had several. Undoubtedly, the moment when David killed Goliath was another defining moment. Things were never the same again for him after that event. It was the best thing that ever happened to David—but it was also the worst thing that ever happened to David. Because the people lavishly praised David, Saul became insanely jealous of him and spent thirteen years pursuing him to take his life.

The distinction between one's defining moment and one's finest hour could be determined by you, the reader. You are therefore free to differ with my choices of what I say is one's defining moment and one's finest hour.

I want this book to make you do more than think. I wrote it to drive you to your knees, so that you might be utterly willing to go outside your comfort zone for the sole glory of God.

I return to the principle from John 5:44 which opened this introduction. Prioritizing the desire for God's honor and glory rather than the admiration of people is wedded to the theme of this book. Jesus asked the Jews of his day:

> How can you believe, since you accept glory from one another but don't seek the glory that comes from the only God?

ONE

Isaac Confirms Jacob against His Personal Will

I blessed him. Indeed, he will be blessed!
—Genesis 27:33

When your will is God's will, you will have your will.
—Charles H. Spurgeon (1834–1892)

I have always felt sorry for people who had famous parents. People either judge, expect too much, or thoughtlessly criticize the children of well-known religious leaders. It seems that people cannot avoid making comparisons. Imagine the pressure on the children of Charles Spurgeon. Or D. L. Moody. Or Martin Luther.

How would you like to grow up being the son of Abraham? Abraham was the patriarch of patriarchs! Isaac would no doubt grow up hearing the complicated story of how his father assumed that Ishmael, Abraham's first-born, was the promised son. For thirteen or more years Abraham sincerely believed that Ishmael was the "offspring" that God had in mind when he gave Abraham the promise of a seed as numerous as the stars of heaven. Abraham was about eighty at that time; his wife Sarah was around seventy and considered beyond the age of child-bearing. But Abraham nonetheless believed what God said, namely, that he would indeed have a son. The result: not only was Abraham counted as righteous (Gen. 15:6), but he was the Apostle Paul's "exhibit A" for the teaching of justification by faith alone (Rom. 4:3–5). Consequently, all who believe the promise of the gospel are considered to be children of Abraham. So, reader, if you believe the gospel, you are a child of Abraham! Not a natural son, like Isaac. Rather, if you believe the gospel, you are a child of Abraham at the level of the Spirit. If we belong to Christ, we are children of Abraham (Gal. 3:29).

Isaac almost certainly grew up knowing he was not his father's firstborn. In ancient Israel the firstborn received double the inheritance. So, it was a big deal knowing you were the first-born. Isaac would have heard how his father was ninety-nine years old when the Lord told him he would have a son by Sarah, who was ninety years old. Abraham fell on his face and laughed when God told him this news. Sarah also laughed to herself when she found out that she would have a son. She did not laugh in exhilaration; her laughter was tinged with unbelief, sarcasm, and irony: "After I am worn out, and my lord is old, shall I have pleasure?" (Gen. 18:12 ESV). Isaac, whose name means "laughter" or "he laughs," would have been told how he got that name, having undoubtedly heard how his mother laughed when she found out she would have a son. He would also have heard how Abraham was not happy when God told him that Ishmael was not the promised child after all (17:18). Isaac was *God's* first choice, but he was Abraham's *second* choice.

When we get to heaven, we will find out just how hard it was for Abraham to say goodbye to Ishmael one day and how his adjusting to the coming of Isaac was a matter of sheer obedience. It was not easy. We do not know if Isaac himself personally grasped this difficult adjustment his father Abraham had to make. But if Isaac understood this, he could have grown up feeling that he was not as loved as Ishmael was. I also wonder if the moment his father was going to sacrifice him to God was a traumatic memory for Isaac. Isaac could never forget this. As the two of them were heading to the spot where Abraham was going to sacrifice him, Isaac said to his father: "Where is the lamb for the burnt offering?" (22:7).

At what stage Isaac would become self-conscious that he was God's first choice but Abraham's second choice is not known. Not that anything would take God by surprise! But Isaac might have been curious about these events. We do know that Abraham had other wives and other sons but gave all he had to Isaac (25:5). I make this observation partly because it seems to me that Isaac was one of the most lackluster persons among the better-known Old Testament people. Isaac might not have thought of the idea of a "place in history." But he almost certainly would have wanted to make his father proud. What was it about Isaac that earned him a place in the Hebrews 11 "hall of faith"? I doubt this was determined by comparing him with his father. Was it the wells he dug—or dug again after they apparently became of no use (cf. Gen. 26:18–19)? Was it his wealth, that he became rich like Abraham (cf. vv. 12–14)? No. "By faith Isaac blessed Jacob and Esau concerning things to come" (Heb.

11:20). So what? Why was this significant? The truth is, as we will see, Hebrews 11:20 describes Isaac's finest hour. I will try to demonstrate why this was significant.

Sarah died when Isaac was thirty-seven years old. Shortly afterward, Abraham needed to get a wife for Isaac. The lengthy story of Abraham's servant finding Rebekah is one of the most beautiful and amazing stories in the Old Testament. Isaac was forty years old when he married Rebekah. The account ends with the observation that when Isaac and Rebekah met, Isaac was "comforted after his mother's death" (Gen. 24:67). That sentence reminds us that Isaac was not merely part of theological history. He was a human being, with feelings. The reference to Isaac in the great faith chapter—Hebrews 11:20—shows simultaneously his greatest disappointment and finest hour.

This is not to say that Isaac's life had no significance. In his one hundred and eighty years, he followed in the steps of his father. First, God renewed to Isaac the promise he gave to Abraham: "The Lord appeared to him and said: 'Do not go down to Egypt. . . . [S]ojourn in this land, and I will be with you and will bless you, for to you and to your offspring I will give all these lands, and I will establish the oath that I swore to Abraham your father'" (Gen. 26:2–3 ESV). Second, Isaac sadly lied about his wife Rebekah by telling the men of Gerar, "She is my sister," because he feared for his life (vv. 6–9). Third, like his father, Isaac became very wealthy and was envied by his neighbors (vv. 12–16). Fourth, he dug wells that had been started by his father Abraham. He became well known for the wells he dug (vv. 17–22). Fifth, God appeared to Isaac just like he did to Abraham, renewing the promise: "I am with you. I will bless you and multiply your offspring because of my servant Abraham"

(v. 24). One thing was apparently not renewed: God did not swear an oath to Isaac. This is not to say it didn't happen. Fifth, like his mother Sarah, who was barren for many years, Isaac's wife Rebekah was also initially barren.

There appears to be a pattern throughout Holy Scripture that some of God's chosen people are kept from having children. One could say God sometimes strategically and sovereignly closes the womb of his choice servants. He closed the womb of Sarah (Gen. 11:30), Rachel (30:1), Hannah, the mother of the prophet Samuel (1 Sam. 1–2), and Elizabeth, mother of John the Baptist (Luke 1:7–13). We can be sure that all of these would-be parents prayed earnestly and fervently to the Lord for children.

So, we are told these words: Isaac prayed. Indeed, "Isaac prayed to the Lord on behalf of his wife because she was childless" (Gen. 25:21).

Consider the stature of people I am talking about. I'm sure that Abraham prayed. We know Isaac prayed. I'm sure Jacob prayed. These are major players! These are as high profile in the kingdom of God as you can get! And yet they needed to pray before their children were born!

These things said, the life of Isaac is not filled with accomplishments when we compare it to Abraham's. Of course, we know about the promise and drama that eventually led to Isaac's birth. We also know that he was nearly sacrificed. But we do know one important thing that Isaac did: he prayed for his childless wife.

Rebekah conceived. And we now enter one of the strangest and most difficult to understand scenarios in the entire Bible. The children struggled in Rebekah's womb. She, of course, was conscious of this. "Why is this happening to me?" she asked.

So now Rebekah prays. First, Isaac prayed. This time Rebekah does. We might speculate and ask: If Isaac had prayed and the Lord answered as he did to Rebekah, would things have turned out differently? Would Isaac have felt differently about Jacob? We will never know. But we do know this: the Lord answered Rebekah.

> Two nations are in your womb;
> two peoples will come from you and be separated.
> One people will be stronger than the other,
> and the older will serve the younger. (v. 23)

This word to Rebekah is undoubtedly one of the most pivotal words in the entire Bible. It not only prophesied the future of the two sons but the future of the nation of Israel. There is more: it would anticipate the most controversial issue in the history of theology; the doctrine of predestination is born here. It is unfolded in Romans chapter nine, which refers back to this passage.

We might well assume that Rebekah told this prophetic word to Isaac. But we don't know for sure. That is one mystery among others from this part of Scripture. I would think that if she had not told Isaac about the Lord's word, they wouldn't have had a great marriage. However, if she did tell him, would this explain to Isaac why she favored Jacob?

Rebekah's divine revelation was followed by the evidence of the prophecy: "there were indeed twins in her womb." I might add: surprise, surprise. But it is important to remember that when one truly receives a prophetic word from the Holy Spirit, verification is certain and definite.

May I give a pastoral word here? If you have a word from God, it will come to pass. If you think that you have a word from God but it does not turn out right, this is no disgrace. Such a situation happens to many of us. But it is disgraceful when you share what you think is a word from God with someone without verifying it and then failing to admit that you got it wrong. Forgive me, but I believe this is a disgrace! My loving advice is: never say "the Lord told me." You can make the Lord look bad even though it is not his fault. Don't claim to speak for the Lord. Simply say, "I feel I may have a word from the Lord." In doing so, you might save yourself untold embarrassment; besides, you will avoid bringing disgrace upon the name of the Lord. Our pride so often leads us to claim to speak for God.

So, God's word to Rebekah was verified: she had twins. There is more:

> The first came out red, all his body like a hairy cloak, so they called his name Esau. Afterward his brother came out with his hand holding Esau's heel, so his name was called Jacob. (vv. 25–26 ESV)

Esau came out first. He was the older, the firstborn, who would normally receive double the inheritance. For some reason, God wanted to reverse that order once more, as he had done with Ishmael and Isaac. The older would be subservient to the younger. The Lord had made this decision before they were born.

As the boys grew up, each parent had a favorite. This is not a good thing—parents should not show favoritism. Esau became a skilled hunter and was a man of the field, while Jacob was a quiet man, dwelling in tents. "Isaac loved Esau because he had a taste for wild game, but Rebekah loved Jacob" (v. 28).

We might wonder if Rebekah told Jacob that she preferred him. In any case, Jacob had plans and seized an opportunity. He thought that Esau selling his birthright to him was the next step forward. Or perhaps the idea came unexpectedly. One day:

> Jacob was cooking a stew [and] Esau came in from the field exhausted. He said to Jacob, "Let me eat some of that red stuff, because I'm exhausted." . . .
>
> Jacob replied, "First sell me your birthright."
>
> "Look," said Esau, "I'm about to die, so what good is a birthright to me?"
>
> Jacob said, "Swear to me first." So he swore to Jacob and sold his birthright to him. Then Jacob gave bread and lentil stew to Esau; he ate, drank, got up, and went away. So Esau despised his birthright. (vv. 29–34)

ISAAC'S MAJOR TEST AND FINEST HOUR

As the time approached for the aged and blind Isaac to bestow his patriarchal blessing (Gen. 27), he summoned Esau. Isaac asked Esau to prepare a special meal for him. Whether Isaac planned to also give a blessing to Jacob is not known. But Rebekah overheard Isaac give these instructions to Esau. She quickly summoned

Jacob, informing him that his father Isaac was about to give his priceless patriarchal blessing to Esau. Rebekah wanted Jacob to receive this blessing instead. She volunteered to prepare the food just as her husband Isaac liked it. She told Jacob to put Esau's garments on. She got him to put skins of young goats on his hands and the smooth part of his neck. Finally, she put the delicious food and bread into Jacob's hands.

Jacob went to his father. He immediately began lying to Isaac.

Isaac, unable to see, asked Jacob, "Who are you?"

Jacob replied, "I am Esau, your firstborn."

Isaac was surprised that the game was found and cooked so quickly. "Because the LORD your God made it happen for me," Jacob replied.

Isaac felt his son. "The voice is the voice of Jacob, but the hands are the hands of Esau." So Isaac proceeded to bless Jacob, but, to be sure, asked: "Are you really my son Esau?"

Jacob continued lying: "I am."

Jacob brought the food and wine. Isaac ate and drank. He said to Jacob, "Please come closer and kiss me, my son." Jacob did. Isaac smelled his garments and blessed him, saying:

> See, the smell of my son
>   is as the smell of a field that the LORD has blessed!
> May God give you of the dew of heaven
>   and of the fatness of the earth
>   and plenty of grain and wine.
> Let peoples serve you,
>   and nations bow down to you.
> Be lord over your brothers,

and may your mother's sons bow down to you.
Cursed be everyone who curses you,
and blessed be everyone who blesses you!
(vv. 27–29 ESV)

At that moment Esau came in from his hunting and brought delicious food for his father. Esau said to his father Isaac, "Let my father get up and eat some of his son's game, so that you may bless me."

The old man was stunned and startled beyond anything he would dream. Isaac's worst nightmare was happening.

"Who are you?" Isaac asked.

"I am Esau your firstborn son," Esau answered.

Then Isaac trembled violently. "Who was it then who hunted game and brought it to me? I ate it all before you came in." Then came the moment—the utterance from Isaac, the pronouncement and word that would not be taken back:

I blessed him. Indeed, he will be blessed! (v. 33)

This was Isaac's finest hour. It was his most self-effacing moment.

Isaac affirmed the blessing and would not take it back. Though he preferred Esau, he demonstrated that he was putting God first. As his father Abraham did not hang on to Ishmael but chose Isaac, now Isaac himself was demonstrating his love for God. It was an extremely hard moment, because he despised the way Rebekah and Jacob had connived to deprive Esau of the patriarchal blessing.

This was the greatest disappointment of Isaac's life. But he accepted God's will. He was resigned to the situation, knowing that the hand of God was on it despite his humiliation through the strange conspiracy of Rebekah and Jacob. But here is the big thing: by faith Isaac pleased God. Isaac did not accomplish much in his own lifetime. But, despite his pain, he went out in a blaze of glory in God's sight. And I suspect that is why his name appears in Hebrews 11:20.

> God moves in a mysterious way
> His wonders to perform.
>
> —William Cowper (1731–1800)

TWO

Leah and Delayed Significance

This time I will praise the L*ORD.*

—Genesis 29:35

Heartache forces us to embrace God out of desperate, urgent need. God is never closer than when your heart is aching.

—Joni Eareckson Tada

It ain't over 'til it's over.

—Yogi Berra (1925–2015)

I once listened to a talk by Susie Hawkins on the subject of Leah entitled "The Unloved Woman." Leah was the perfect example of an unloved woman—both her father and her husband saw her as a step, a means to an end. They did not have the slightest regard for her feelings. Life was constant humiliation for Leah. Scripture gives no hint that anybody around her cared—neither

her father, her husband, nor her sister. There are countless women, married and unmarried, young and old, rich and poor, who know what it is like to be treated with contempt by a father and a husband. Some women are mistreated by their children, or even grandchildren. Some are abused by employers, relatives, or authority figures. Most of these women have no thought or hope of vindication or significance. In fact, I doubt Leah had such a thought, much less a hope.

Do you crave vindication, appreciation, or affirmation in your life right now?

All of us are born with a need for significance. God made us this way. Significance means importance: the quality of being worthy of attention.

A strain runs right through the Bible showing how God is for the underdog. God was for Leah, just as Jesus was for the woman found in adultery (John 8:1–8). God showed sympathy for sinners and anger toward the self-righteous, always hearing the cries of the poor, those in prison (Heb. 13:3), and the neglected Christians in Jerusalem who were abused by wealthy believers (James 5:1–5).

Similarly, the need for vindication is common for many. To be vindicated means having your name cleared; to be absolved from blame, to be proved to be right. Having vindication, affirmation, or appreciation withheld can be one of the most painful ordeals a human being ever goes through.

Leah was a person who desired vindication. Because Jacob clearly loved Leah's sister, it was humiliating for Leah to be Jacob's first bride. I don't see where she got any sympathy or appreciation in that episode.

Do you know what the pain of being unappreciated feels

like? Are you in a difficult ordeal now? Have you been set aside so that you feel insignificant?

There is not a human being ever born that did not grow up wanting to feel affirmed or appreciated—to feel a sense of significance. As I said, this is the way God made us.

For many years—twenty-two, to be exact—all I lived for was vindication. Or affirmation, significance. In 1956, a theological decision I made greatly displeased my father and grandmother. It also understandably caused members of my old denomination to distance themselves from me. My father and grandmother were godly Christians—they meant no harm but wanted me to be on the right path. My grandmother had purchased a brand new 1955 Chevrolet for me to drive between Nashville and Palmer, Tennessee, when I was a student pastor at Trevecca Nazarene College (now University), but took it back when my theology surprisingly changed. My dad even said, "Son, you have broken with God." I knew I hadn't, but I had nothing to show for my new direction in life.

I was in "no man's land" for a long time. I worked as a baby equipment salesman, a life insurance salesman, and a door-to-door vacuum cleaner salesman from 1956 to 1973. I was preaching in different places and denominations over those years—including paying for my own radio broadcast—but this did not impress my friends and relatives in the slightest. However, when my father learned that I had become pastor of the same church that Dr. G. Campbell Morgan had pastored—Westminster Chapel—he visited me. On a train from Edinburgh, Scotland, to King's Cross Station in London in 1978, my father looked at me and said, "Son, I'm proud of you. You were right and I was wrong." I was happy to hear those words, of course!

It was wonderful to hear my father's approval, which I had craved for years. But my desire for my father's approval diminished as my vindication in the Spirit increased. I knew without any doubt that God was with me. Jesus, after all, was vindicated by the Spirit (1 Tim. 3:16).

Jacob, similarly, went through a period of family separation. After all, he stole both Esau's birthright and patriarchal blessing. When Rebekah learned that Esau was now determined to kill Jacob, she warned Jacob to leave immediately and go to the home of her brother Laban in Haran. Isaac also urged Jacob to go there.

On his way to Laban's, Jacob experienced the well-known dream of a ladder that reached to heaven. Angels of God were ascending and descending on it. God said to Jacob:

> I am the LORD, the God of Abraham your father and the God of Isaac. The land on which you lie I will give to you and to your offspring. Your offspring shall be like the dust of the earth, and you shall spread abroad to the west and to the east and to the north and to the south, and in you and your offspring shall all the families of the earth be blessed. Behold, I am with you and will keep you wherever you go, and will bring you back to this land. For I will not leave you until I have done what I have promised you. (Gen. 28:13–15 ESV)

Jacob eventually came to the area in which Laban lived (Gen. 29). He asked people if they knew Laban. They did—in fact, Laban's daughter Rachel was coming to the well at that moment with sheep. When Jacob saw Rachel, he loved her at first sight. Jacob kissed her in Middle Eastern fashion (on both cheeks) and began to weep aloud. Rachel ran to tell her father Laban, who welcomed Jacob openly and warmly.

After Jacob had stayed there a month, he and Laban came to an agreement on Jacob's wages. Jacob said, "I'll work for you seven years for your younger daughter Rachel." Laban agreed. Jacob served seven years for Rachel, and they seemed to him but a few days "because of his love for her" (29:20).

But Laban had two daughters. And Rachel was Laban's younger daughter. The older daughter, Leah, was not yet married. A curious description of Leah is that her eyes were "weak" (v. 17 NIV). Interpreters over the centuries have been puzzled over this description. I won't add to the confusion. Whatever the meaning of "weak" with reference to Leah, I believe it simply serves to contrast how Jacob perceived Rachel, who was "beautiful." The point was that Jacob had eyes only for Rachel.

At this point a turn happened in the narrative, and it turned out to be traumatic for Jacob, Rachel, and Leah. Did Laban prepare his daughters for the events of the coming days? We are not told. Jacob's seven years were up, so he went to Laban and said, "Since my time is complete, give me my wife, so I can sleep with her." So Laban gathered the people together and made a feast. Apparently, Jacob was now in the dark tent and was waiting for Rachel to come inside. There evidently were no lights, and the bride would be heavily veiled. Laban brought Leah—not Rachel—into the tent. When they woke up in the morning, lo and behold, "there was Leah!"

This was cruel of Laban. First, he was cruel to Leah. This was against her will. How do you suppose she felt? She would have known how Jacob felt about Rachel. She would have known that Jacob could have chosen her had he been attracted to her, but he obviously wasn't. She would have been humiliated to see the look on Jacob's face the next day. She must have dreaded that moment with all her being. Had Laban no thoughts or feelings for his beloved daughter Leah?

Second, this event was traumatic for Jacob. The moment he looked forward to for seven years had arrived. But he had been wedded to Leah and not to Rachel. "Why have you deceived me?" Jacob angrily asked Laban.

In so many words, Laban said: "Oh, sorry about that." He then explained: "It is not the custom in our country to give the younger daughter in marriage before the firstborn." By what we learn of Laban's character later, it is not surprising that he had made this excuse up. He then said to Jacob that he should complete the week of wedding celebration and that Jacob would get Rachel, but he would then have to serve Laban another seven years!

Leah's hurt was being walked over by her own father on the night of her wedding.

But that was just the beginning of Leah's being unloved.

Nevertheless, something good was coming for Leah and something not so good was coming for Rachel.

This is the moment that we all need to be reminded that God gives and also withholds life. What follows is a reminder that God is in control. Indeed, "When the Lord saw that Leah was neglected, he opened her womb; but Rachel was unable to conceive" (v. 31).

So, although Jacob had two wives, only one of them could conceive. This is the moment when we discover that Leah had a relationship with God and was undoubtedly praying all this time. Leah conceived and bore a son. She (not Jacob) called his name Reuben, because "the LORD has looked upon my affliction." Leah then added, hopefully, "for now my husband will love me" (v. 32 ESV). Did she regard her "weak eyes" as an affliction? Possibly. But her hope that a son would turn Jacob's heart toward her was too optimistic. Sadly, it made no difference.

Then Leah conceived again and another baby came along. She had been praying about all this.

Leah was always aware that God was watching: "The LORD heard that I am neglected and has given me this son also." She called this second son Simeon (v. 33). Lo and behold, Leah hadn't given up the hope that having sons would change Jacob.

Another baby came—yet another boy! "At last, my husband will become attached to me, because I have borne three sons for him," declared Leah, naming the baby Levi (v. 34).

I suspect that Leah was counting on Jacob to see for himself that God was behind her having sons. After all, she was not only bearing children; they were *males*. Leah hoped that God blessing her in this way would surely have a deep influence on Jacob and cause him to see that God was at the bottom of her success in having sons. Not only that, but Leah was counting on Jacob's own male pride and virility having a positive influence on his self-esteem. Furthermore, Leah having sons would surely cause Jacob to appreciate her. During all this time his beautiful Rachel was barren. Did any of this change Jacob? No, it did not. Would Leah then have another son? Would she keep hoping that another male child would finally shift his affection toward her?

Then came a fourth son from Leah—Judah. We have reached the stage where we witness Leah's finest hour. We also learn how special her relationship to God was. We know how God was tenderly looking on Leah. Leah now made a decision; it was the greatest decision of her life. Instead of trying to change Jacob, moralizing him, or nagging him, she entered a new world. Leah gave up on Jacob. She uttered some of the most moving words in the entire Bible:

> This time I will praise the LORD. (v. 35)

This was Leah's finest hour. It was an amazing, wonderful, and glorious decision. She gave up on trying to win Jacob over to her. She now had a different goal, a different aim, and a different plan. It was not a new strategy to win Jacob over, nor was it doing anything to appeal to Jacob at all. Leah had an entirely new outlook. Jacob, in fact, was now out of the picture.

Leah made the greatest, profoundest, wisest, and most God-honoring decision she could make even if she had been able to take a thousand years to come up with it. It was a paradigm shift. Nothing would ever be the same for Leah again. But neither would she be appreciated by her husband—ever. Thankfully, she now had peace.

Moreover, not only was God behind Leah's decision; he was keeping Jacob from showing affection, admiration, and preference for her. This was God's providential strategy all along. God was behind Leah's affliction and disappointment because he wanted her attention. He got it. God won—and Leah won.

But what about significance? *Leah finally got that, too*! No one ever—ever—commits themselves to God like Leah did without the greatest inner satisfaction imaginable. Peace. Joy. God's own presence. Contentment. Pleasure and praise that comes from the only God (John 5:44). This amazing feeling cannot be imitated. We cannot make it up. It is called the "joy of the LORD" (Neh.

8:10). Leah would experience what would be said of Jesus Christ centuries later: he was vindicated in the Spirit (1 Tim. 3:16). There are two kinds of vindication: (1) external—when all see the truth; and (2) internal—when no person sees God's pleasure and approval, but you sense it.

There is another consideration no one thought of at the time of these four boys' births. There was a level of significance for Leah, appreciation and vindication for her that outweighs, outlasts, and outdistances any kind of measurement that one would have grasped: historical significance. I am talking about Leah's legacy, with particular reference to two of those sons.

"It ain't over 'til it's over."

LEVI

Leah initially gave birth to four sons. Two of these—Levi and Judah—would have major and eternal significance upon Israel, the church, and the world. Down the road came the tribe of Levi. Years later the tribe of Levi would produce the greatest man in the Old Testament—Moses. Moses was that greatest man between Adam and Jesus. He led the children of Israel out of Egypt and across the Red Sea on dry land. But at Mount Sinai the children of Israel rebelled against Moses when he confronted them about the golden calf they had built. He then cried out to all twelve tribes: "Whoever is for the LORD, come to me." In response, the sons of *Levi* gathered around him. As a consequence of this moment, the tribe of Levi was ordained for the service of the Lord (Ex. 32:26–29). The priesthood, the instructions in the book of Leviticus, the law, and the sacrificial system that pointed to the death of Jesus were all under the jurisdiction of the Levites. Moses, the priesthood, and the law are thus a legacy of Leah.

Would Leah realize this? No. Would she have surmised anything like this? No. All her suffering, sense of insignificance, and withheld appreciation would seem to be of no value. But her glory—though hidden from her—would be unveiled in subsequent history and in eternal glory.

The legacy of Judah, however, was even greater.

JUDAH

Leah's fourth son would turn out to be the greatest of the twelve sons of Jacob (later called Israel). It was none other than the uncaring and heartless Jacob who gave this prophecy concerning his son Judah:

> Judah, your brothers shall praise you;
> your hand shall be on the neck of your enemies;
> your father's sons shall bow down before you.
> Judah is a lion's cub;
> from the prey, my son, you have gone up.
> He stooped down; he crouched as a lion
> and as a lioness; who dares rouse him?
> The scepter shall not depart from Judah,
> nor the ruler's staff from between his feet,
> until tribute comes to him;
> and to him shall be the obedience of the peoples.
> Binding his foal to the vine
> and his donkey's colt to the choice vine,

he has washed his garments in wine
and his vesture in the blood of grapes.
His eyes are darker than wine,
and his teeth whiter than milk.
(Gen. 49:8–12 ESV)

The eventual offspring of Judah was David—Israel's greatest king. Consider the genealogy of Jesus:

> The book of the genealogy of Jesus Christ, the son of David, the son of Abraham.
>
> Abraham was the father of Isaac, and Isaac the father of Jacob, and Jacob the father of Judah and his brothers . . . and David was the father of Solomon by the wife of Uriah . . . and Jacob the father of Joseph the husband of Mary, of whom Jesus was born, who is called Christ. (Matt. 1:1–2, 6, 16 ESV)

Years later the Apostle John on the isle of Patmos saw a vision:

> I saw a mighty angel proclaiming with a loud voice, "Who is worthy to open the scroll and break its seals?" . . . And one of the elders said to me, "Weep no more; behold, the Lion of the tribe of Judah, the Root of David, has conquered, so that he can open the scroll and its seven seals." (Rev. 5:2, 5 ESV)

One more thing: Levi and Judah met in Jesus Christ. Jesus, the Lion of the tribe of Judah, fulfilled the law of Moses that came from the tribe of Levi. Jesus had promised to fulfill this law (Matt. 5:17) and did so when he uttered the words "It is finished" on the cross (John 19:30). This remarkable story began when an insensitive father led an insignificant woman to marry an unworthy man.

Leah's feelings at one time could easily be summed up in the words of David: "No one cares for my soul" (Ps. 142:4 ESV). Feeling utterly insignificant, Leah had no idea that she was making redemptive history when she gave birth to her fourth son, Judah. And yet that was when she had her finest hour by saying, "This time I will praise the Lord." Leah will be the most surprised person in heaven when she learns that she was an essential part in the eternal plan of God. But I suspect that *all* of us will be surprised that we were used of God. "When did we see you sick, or in prison, and visit you?" (Matt. 25:39), we will say.

Leah would not live to see what was down the road for these two sons, but in history and in heaven she will receive greater honor than her beautiful sister Rachel. Leah had no glory or satisfaction on her wedding night with Jacob. She had no happiness in her marriage. She was an unloved woman on earth. But one day she will be loved, admired, appreciated, honored, and vindicated beyond her most imaginative fancies.

When my mother died at the age of forty-three (I was seventeen), I was one grieved, sorrowful, and weeping teenager. I have never gotten over it. But I was comforted in hearing a song by Esther Rusthoi, "It Will Be Worth It All," declaring how our suffering will seem so insignificant when we see Jesus.

Paul said, "I consider that the sufferings of this present time are not worth comparing with the glory that is to be revealed to us" (Rom. 8:18 ESV). Are you unloved? It ain't over 'til it's over. And it won't be over until we are in heaven and see Jesus face to face.

It will be worth it all when we see Jesus.

THREE

Joshua and Letting God Be God

When Joshua was near Jericho, he looked up and saw a man standing in front of him with a drawn sword in his hand. Joshua approached him and asked, "Are you for us or for our adversaries?"

"Neither," he replied, "I have now come as commander of the LORD's army."

Then Joshua bowed with his face to the ground in homage and asked him, "What does my lord want to say to his servant?"

The commander of the LORD's army said to Joshua, "Remove the sandals from your feet, for the place where you are standing is holy." And Joshua did that.

—Joshua 5:13–15

My willingness to forsake any claim upon God is the only evidence that I have seen the Divine glory.

—N. Burnette Magruder (1914–2005)

I was ordained to the Christian ministry at the Thirteenth Street Baptist Church in Ashland, Kentucky, on November 15, 1964. The preacher was one of my earliest mentors, Dr. N. B. Magruder. He shaped my theology and understanding of God more than anyone. Dr. Magruder asked me a number of heavy questions in front of a congregation of three hundred. My wife Louise, my father, and my grandmother were present. It was not a very pleasant evening. I had no way of knowing the questions Dr. Magruder would ask. As the questioning went on, my confidence sunk. I believed then and believe now that my teaching had been revealed to me by the Holy Spirit. But Dr. Magruder took me to a level for which I was not prepared. He asked me to explain the Trinity in the Old Testament. I thought he was my friend! What was happening? Nobody can explain the Trinity in the New or Old Testaments, so maybe that was an unfair question. I had become overconfident, if not arrogant, because I felt I knew with certainty what I believed and preached. Dr. Magruder finally asked what is the *one word* that would be the sum total of all of God's attributes. I did not know—I was flummoxed and embarrassed. But this experience was good for me.

When a person becomes a Christian, he or she has little or no idea what to expect in days to come. The three thousand who were converted on the day of Pentecost were given no "follow-up," as it is sometimes called. There was no preparation for their being baptized. They were baptized the same day they received the Gospel. When Philip led the Ethiopian to the Lord, there was no preparation for his baptism—nor was there any follow-up. Philip simply disappeared (Acts 8:36–39). A Christian is not normally cautioned, "Be ready for the hiding of God's face, as this event will surely come." One is not usually told to watch out lest you become overly familiar with God. In any case, would instructions like these be all that helpful? Maybe—or maybe not. In my opinion, although I would urge follow-up—the more the better—each Christian must eventually learn for himself or herself. Furthermore, many Christians reach a point in their lives when they feel God lets them down. Some feel betrayed by God—they hit a wall. Some break through the wall and discover how real God is. But others don't. Nevertheless, we must all sooner or later break the betrayal barrier. The breaking of this barrier comes by persistent faith, by not giving up. So, the Christian life is full of surprises, sudden challenges, and disappointments.

Joshua was the successor to Moses. His job was to lead the children of Israel into the land of Canaan—the land flowing with milk and honey. His initiation into this land was to see a formidable, threatening figure—an angel—who was the commander of the Lord's army but who was not taking sides with regard to Israel's future enemies. God *always* took sides against Israel's enemies, but this new figure strangely did not choose either side. Joshua's finest hour came when he was instantly willing to accept this commander's surprising word. It meant knowing God at a new level for which he had not been prepared.

Joshua had been loyal to God and to everything he was taught by Moses. He and Caleb had voted long before that the children of Israel should go into Canaan during the beginning of their sojourn in the wilderness. But Joshua and Caleb were outvoted—ten tribes to two (Num. 13–14). They fought spiritual and physical warfare for forty years in the desert—defeating Israel's enemies right, left, and center. God had always been on Israel's side all this time. Toward the end of Moses's life, he laid his hands on Joshua, who thus became Moses's successor. "Joshua son of Nun was filled with the spirit of wisdom because Moses had laid his hands on him" (Deut. 34:9). After Moses died, God said to Joshua,

> I have given you every place where the sole of your foot treads, just as I promised Moses . . . I will be with you, just as I was with Moses. I will not leave you or abandon you.
>
> Be strong and courageous, for you will distribute the land I swore to their ancestors to give them as an inheritance. (Josh. 1:3, 5–6)

Then came the day that Joshua announced to the children of Israel that the time had come to enter Canaan. These were the children of the parents of the original generation. Because their parents had sided with the majority against Joshua and Caleb nearly forty years before, God swore in his wrath that they would never be allowed to enter Canaan (Heb. 3:10–11). Indeed, all these rebels had died in the wilderness except for Joshua and Caleb. Now at last Joshua could announce: "When you see the ark of the covenant of the LORD your God carried by the Levitical priests, you are to break camp and follow it" (Josh. 3:3). The Israelites miraculously crossed over the Jordan River, repeating the miracle of crossing the Red Sea.

When Joshua crossed over the Jordan River with the children of Israel, he was unexpectedly confronted with a situation for which he was not prepared—the awesome, scary figure standing before him with a drawn sword in his hand. This did not appear to be a friendly encounter! Joshua asked him, "Are you for us or for our enemies?" The reply: "No." (Some versions say: "Neither.") The mysterious figure added: "I have now come as commander of the LORD's army" (5:14).

These words were likely initially disappointing news for Joshua to hear. He might have seen this as a betrayal! Had he done something wrong? What caused God to change his mind and suddenly not be with Joshua and the children of Israel?

The commander of the Lord's army was an angel utterly devoted to God and no one else. Joshua instantly discerned that this angel had come to take over. The Lord's army, furthermore, would consist of countless angels who would fight the battles—from dismantling the walls of Jericho to destroying Ai. Hundreds of years later the prophet Elisha would comment in a major battle, "Those who are with us outnumber those who are with them" (2 Kings 6:16).

It is a sign of true spirituality when one recognizes the presence of God. Because Joshua was filled with the Spirit, he knew that the angel was directed by the true God.

But why did this angel appear to be against Israel by not taking sides? Why did the angel say "No" (or "Neither")? It was because *the angel was only on God's side*. Joshua needed to learn—as you and I do—*that no one has a claim upon God*. Earlier, God had said to Moses that he would have compassion on whom he would have compassion (Ex. 33:19). We do not tell God what to do; he tells us what to do. We do not have any authority or any right to instruct him. God does not exist for us; he exists for himself—for his own glory. He is a jealous God; his name is Jealous (34:14). God did not create himself or make himself this way; this is the way he is, was, and always will be. He does not need us. He existed without us before the world began—before there was a star, an angel, a planet, or a speck of dust. He is *before* all things and, having *chosen to create*, he holds all things together (Col. 1:17). The angel was not on Joshua's side; he was on God's side. Or, as Martin Luther would put it, we must know God as an enemy before we can know him as a friend.

As I mentioned earlier, I believe that every Christian must eventually break through a betrayal barrier. God sometimes appears to betray us. He hides his face from us. He does not always answer our prayers. He allows best friends to desert us. He lets us become seriously ill. He allows financial reverse. Many Christians are tempted to respond by giving up rather than persisting in faith. That is what happened to the children of Israel in the wilderness. They were intimidated by the inhabitants of Canaan, saying, "We seemed like grasshoppers" (Num. 13:33). They utterly gave up. They were not far from Canaan and could have entered into their inheritance. But because of that unbelief, they would never—ever—know the manifested power of God.

Reader, do you feel betrayed by God? If you look at the lives of those described in Hebrews 11, you will find that they knew what it was like to feel betrayed by God. Nevertheless, they persisted. Those who had their "finest hour" as shown in this book had this in common: they broke the betrayal barrier.

Joshua undoubtedly had developed a true and solid intimacy with God under the tutorage of Moses. God had been very real to Joshua. But Joshua still needed to learn that he did not have any permanent "rights" with God: he could never tell God what to do. Many of us are in danger of unwittingly and unconsciously developing an overfamiliarity with God. God knows this about all of us; the heart is deceitful above all things and incurably wicked (Jer. 17:9). God knows our frame; he remembers that we are dust (Ps. 103:13–14).

Thankfully, God protects us from ourselves. It is for our good that he hides his face from us from time to time lest we act like we own him or can tell him what to do. God does us no favor to let us go on and on in arguing with him instead of putting us in our place. Otherwise we could cease to worship God with awe; we might think we could snap our fingers and expect him to jump.

This is the lesson Joshua needed to learn.

The angel's effect on Joshua was overwhelming. It was simultaneous shock, disappointment, and utter worship. There was much for him to absorb. His initial reaction was almost certainly an inability to figure out what this meant. Joshua at first got a letdown unlike anything he had ever experienced. To him this experience did not add up with what he had heard before. God had promised Joshua that every foot of ground he stepped on would be his. God had appointed Joshua as Moses's successor. God had said to Joshua that he would be with him as he was with Moses. The land of Canaan had been promised. So how could this scary angel say "No" (or "Neither")?

Answer: Joshua had more to learn about God's ways.

In the end, this would be Joshua's finest hour. Joshua was being brought to a new and higher level of knowing and understanding God. Although Joshua was not expecting anything like this, he nonetheless showed that he was not only open to a greater revelation of the God of glory, but he was utterly submissive to him. He responded by "[bowing] with his face to the ground." As Saul of Tarsus would be knocked to the ground well over a thousand years later and say, "What should I do, Lord?"

(Acts 22:10), so Joshua asked: "What does my lord want to say to his servant?" Instead of shaking his fist and yelling, "How could you do this to me?" Joshua humbly said, "What does my lord want to say to his servant?"

The austere man with the drawn sword turned out to be Joshua's friend, not his enemy. But because the angel—who existed only for the glory of God—said "No" (or "Neither") to Joshua, he found out how wonderful, tender, and precious God is. The commander of the Lord's army said to Joshua, "Remove the sandals from your feet, for the place where you are standing is holy ground." And Joshua did so, just as Moses had many years before when he had been commanded to take off his shoes at the burning bush (Ex. 3:5).

I see this occasion of Joshua and the commander of the Lord's army as a reminder that we all have more to learn about God. I suspect, too, that we all need to be reminded of our weaknesses and depravity. After all, if we say we have no sin, we deceive ourselves and the truth is not in us (1 John 1:8). It takes seeing the glory of God for us to see more fully our sinfulness. We should pray with David:

> Search me, God, and know my heart;
> test me and know my concerns.
> See if there is any offensive way in me;
> lead me in the everlasting way. (Ps. 139:23–24)

I remember sitting on the front row of the Thirteenth Street Baptist Church before a service with Dr. N. B. Magruder and saying to him, "I reckon that the greatest way we can show devotion to God is to be a martyr for the Lord. Would you agree?" He smiled, took out a pen and paper, and wrote. Then he handed the note to me. I have carried it with me for years and years and years. It remains the profoundest statement I have ever heard in my lifetime other than what is in the Bible:

> My willingness to forsake any claim upon God is the only evidence that I have seen the Divine glory.

It took me years to grasp this. I still am in awe of it. The statement does not only say that "God owes me nothing" but that I am *happy* about this. I am totally compliant. Jonathan Edwards taught us that the one thing the devil cannot produce in us is a love for the glory of God. Therefore, if you truly love the glory of God, this is a sure sign of God's grace at work in you. You are loving God for being just like he is; loving him and knowing him for his own sake. This way of viewing God is the polar opposite to the way so many Christians think about God nowadays.

There is something innate in all of us suggesting that God owes us something. We presumably have a claim upon God. We can demand certain things. We have rights. On the contrary, I believe that one of the worst things characterizing today's generation is a sense of entitlement. We feel this way toward the government. We feel this way toward our parents. Our educational system. Our employers. The church. And, ultimately, God.

Consider all the attributes of the God of the Bible: he is omnipotent, omniscient, omnipresent, just, loving, sovereign, and holy. The one word that says each of these in one stroke: *glory*. He alone is the "God of glory" (Acts 7:2).

When we truly see the glory of God, we will realize that we have no claim upon God. And when we become utterly willing to forsake any claim upon him, this suggests we have begun to see a glimpse of his glory.

This is what God was teaching Joshua with the angel. It was also what Joshua was most willing to learn, and it equipped him for his task ahead. There is an important caution, however: we can all become self-righteous over our willingness to forsake any claim upon God. Oh, how deceitful the heart is; who can know it? (Jer. 17:9). Can anyone?

FOUR

Habakkuk's Willingness to Wait

Though the fig tree does not bud
and there is no fruit on the vines,
though the olive crop fails
and the fields produce no food,
though the flocks disappear from the pen
and there are no herds in the stalls,
yet I will celebrate in the LORD;
I will rejoice in the God of my salvation!
The LORD my Lord is my strength;
he makes my feet like those of a deer
and enables me to walk on mountain heights!

—Habakkuk 3:17–19

You can save a lot of time waiting on God.

—Adrian Rogers (1931–2005)

The problem of evil is one of the oldest and most difficult questions in human history. Common excuses people give for not believing in God are revealed in statements such as "Why did God create the world knowing that people would suffer?" and "Explain to me why God allows evil when he could stop it, and I will become a Christian." The true reason for unbelief will not be found in answers to these statements, but unsatisfactory answers from Christians are what people claim as reasons to avoid receiving the gospel of Christ.

As I mentioned earlier, I cannot say for sure whether my finest hour has happened. One of my greatest *decisions* happened during my twenty-five years at Westminster Chapel. I invited Arthur Blessitt to spend six Sunday evenings preaching there. It was the most controversial decision I made, and it nearly cost me my ministry at the Chapel. Arthur Blessitt is best known as the man who carried a self-made wooden cross around the world. Some of our more traditional members did not believe it was appropriate for him to preach at Westminster Chapel! The truth is, Arthur Blessitt turned us upside down and changed my life. One of the results of his influence was our Pilot Light ministry, in which we witnessed on the streets of London between Victoria Station, Big Ben, and Buckingham Palace. For the next twenty-five years, I spent a couple of hours nearly every Saturday talking to passersby. What surprised me most was the number of people who thought they were the first to think that the problem of evil and suffering was a good reason to reject salvation in Jesus!

In fact, Habakkuk the Old Testament prophet wrestled with the problem of evil and suffering over twenty-five hundred years ago. He grappled with this dilemma more than any other writer in the Bible. Habakkuk had four complaints with God (Hab. 1:2–4; 12–17), which were his way of saying that God doesn't make sense. Keeping in mind that God is all-powerful and utterly holy, here is a summary of Habakkuk's complaints:

1. Habakkuk's prayers are unanswered—God does not seem to listen.
2. God appears to side with the enemy. He is looking the other way during violence.
3. People still have to endure injustice even though God's eyes are too pure to look on evil.
4. God is tolerating evil even though he is able to stop it.

Thousands of years ago, Habakkuk wanted to know the same thing we all want to know! He wanted God to explain the reason for evil and suffering.

God responded by suggesting to Habakkuk that he go to the spot called the lookout tower ("watchtower," KJV), where he would meet him. Oh good, thought Habakkuk:

> I will stand at my guard post
> and station myself on the lookout tower.
> I will watch to see what he will say to me
> and what I should reply about my complaint. (2:1)

Imagine this. Habakkuk believed he was going to get the answer to the question everybody wants! He could hardly wait. He was also anticipating his own response: "what I should reply about my complaint" (v. 1). But when God showed up, he seemingly kicked the can down the road instead of answering Habakkuk's question:

> The LORD answered me:
>
> Write down this vision;
> clearly inscribe it on tablets
> so one may easily read it.
> For the vision **is yet for the appointed time;**
> **it testifies about the end** and will not lie.
> Though it delays, wait for it,
> Since it will certainly come and not be late. (2:2–3, emphasis mine)

Habakkuk was disappointed. He thought he was going to find out the riddle of riddles—the answer of answers—the explanation of explanations. But God said in so many words, "Not now. The vision is for a future time." What is the vision? It is the revelation that explains why God allows evil and suffering. God knows what we all want to know! He knew what Habakkuk wanted to know. But this knowledge is future. It is down the road, at an appointed time. When? Answer: "the end." "At the end it will speak, and it will not lie" (NKJV). "It speaks of the end" (NIV).

Whatever does "the end" mean? Answer: THE END. It refers to the second coming of Jesus, when every knee shall bow and every tongue confess that Jesus Christ is Lord, to the glory of God the Father (Phil. 2:9–11).

It will be the last day—*when God clears his name.* Then—and not until then—will be the vision—the revelation—the unveiling—the final explanation—of why God chose to create the world and humankind knowing that we all would suffer.

You may be among those who say: *God has a lot to answer for.* I answer: he will. He will explain. He will explain why he allowed death. He will show why he permitted an evil, ugly, horrible, and powerful Satan to bring sin. Suffering. Earthquakes. Hurricanes. Tornados. War. Unjust judges. Sickness. Hurt of every kind. Crazy people inflicting pain on others—to babies—to hungry people.

Did you think that God did not know about these things? Did you think that God did not know that people would use all these evils against him? Was he unaware that all this suffering would be their excuse to refuse to believe in him?

Why? Why does God let the explanation remain hidden? Why—when he could stop it in a second—does he knowingly, purposefully, and deliberately appear to look the other way when such suffering causes the people he created (without their permission) to cry, scream, and feel such pain? Does he not know? Of course he knows. Does he not see? Of course he sees. Then how can a loving, caring, merciful, and omnipotent God live with himself when all this is going on?

I don't know. Habakkuk didn't know. Nobody else on earth knows. But God himself knows. Habakkuk pleaded, could God not tell us now? Of course God could tell us now. But he chose to wait—until the end. He has decided not to clear his name until the end. Yes, the end—there will be an end. There will be an explanation. He will clear his name.

How? The answer is: the revelation will be slow. It will tarry. More people need to be born, for one thing. More people also need to be saved and make up a bride for God's Son—a number which no man could number!

One other thing: God sees the end from the beginning. If so, how can he live with himself during this time? Answer: he will explain this too.

Now Habakkuk has a decision on his hands. Will he accept God's word—to wait? Or will he rebel and say, "I will not worship a God like that"? Deciding to wait, to trust God's timing, and to believe would leave Habakkuk vulnerable, not having satisfactory answers to critically important questions and perhaps looking foolish.

God said more to Habakkuk. First, "Look, his ego is inflated; he is without integrity." This refers to the people who hate God. They refuse to worship a God who has power to stop evil but won't. Second, "the righteous one will live by his faith" (Hab. 2:4). In this profound, powerful, and prophetic verse are these important points particularly about the words "his faith": (1) "his" refers to God's—capital His; (2) "faith" means "faithfulness." The verse should read (and is to be understood this way in the three times it is quoted in the New Testament: Rom. 1:17; Gal. 3:11; Heb. 10:38):

> The righteous shall live by His faithfulness.

The Dead Sea Scrolls commentaries reflect that this is the way the Hebrews understood Habakkuk 2:4: the righteous, or just, shall live by God's faithfulness.

TWO SETS OF TWOS

There are essentially two worldviews when it comes to the nature of faith:

1. **Theodicy:** God is Sovereign Creator with purpose and is in control; he will win in the end and will have the last word.
2. **Existentialism:** there is no purpose, rhyme, nor reason in the universe. Nature or humankind is basically in control and, at best, cooperates with God—as in open theism. (In fact, a leading open theist of our time admitted that God could lose in the end!)

There are also two kinds of faith:

1. **The biblical view:** "Faith is the reality of what is hoped for, the proof of what is not seen" (Heb. 11:1).
2. **The secular/atheist view:** "I will believe it when I see it."

The problem with the secularist view is that believing something when it is seen disqualifies itself as faith. Every eye shall see Jesus in the end, when many shall weep and wail—but at that point it won't be faith.

True faith is when you believe the sheer word of God without the tangible evidence. The atheist, of course, says, "That's crazy; that's insane!" As Christians, we take this retort on the chin and choose to look like fools. But our day will come; we believe that God will clear his name in the end, as Habakkuk is taught.

By the way, whereas only a fool would claim to know why God allows suffering, I can undoubtedly reveal *part* of the reason. *Suffering makes faith possible.* For example, Jesus told his twelve disciples why he did not jump to the cry of Mary and

Martha, who expected Jesus to come at once to heal their brother Lazarus. "So that you may believe," he explained (John 11:15). In other words, if God answers every prayer every time you turn to him, you wouldn't need faith! God's choosing to withhold mercy is what makes faith a possibility. When he allows bad things to happen, you need faith to believe that he exists (Heb. 11:6).

As I said earlier, Habakkuk 2:4 is quoted three times in the New Testament. The quotations in Galatians and Romans refer to relying on the gospel, through which we are given an imputed righteousness. The third quotation, by the writer to the Hebrews, refers to encouraging discouraged believers to not give up but rely on God's faithfulness to keep his word. He is faithful who promised. Thus, living by God's faithfulness is what honors him.

The prophet Habakkuk has to make a decision, and Habakkuk 2:3–4 presents two options. Isaac had to decide whether to let his blessing on Jacob stand or revoke it. Leah had to decide whether to praise the Lord or complain for the rest of her life. Joshua had to decide whether to be offended by the awesome commander of the Lord's armies or worship. Habakkuk had to decide whether to side with the wicked complainers of this world or side with the righteous who would live by God's faithfulness to explain himself in the end.

Habakkuk does not tell us exactly how he came to his decision. But he saw something in the heart of the true God that compelled him to forecast:

> For the earth will be filled
> with the knowledge of the LORD's glory,
> as the water covers the sea. (2:14)

Habakkuk also saw something in the God of glory that encouraged him to pray:

> LORD, I have heard the report about you;
> LORD, I stand in awe of your deeds.
> Revive your work in these years;
> Make it known in these years. (3:2)

There will be two classes of people at the final judgment—on the day God clears his name. The first class will be comprised of those who have been bitter and angry and hateful toward God all their lives—they will get an answer. When God gives the explanation, the answer will be so brilliant and overwhelming that the wisest person there will say, "Why didn't I think of that?" No one in that class will be able to come up with an answer because it was kept hidden by a God of glory to be revealed at the last day. The second class will contain those who had cleared God's name in advance. They are the ones who have already confessed Jesus Christ as Lord to the glory of God the Father! It will be a day of unimaginable joy and ecstasy for those who chose to live by the faithfulness of God when they see and hear him clear his name in his appointed time.

Habakkuk closes his little book without giving everything away. He testifies that he decided to wait for the vision. Habakkuk's willingness to wait until the last day, which was beyond his timeline, was his finest hour. He decided to rejoice and take comfort in the future revelation of God's righteousness more than his own need for answers or the ability to give those answers to others.

Though the fig tree does not bud
and there is no fruit on the vines,
though the olive crop fails
and the fields produce no food,
though the flocks disappear from the pen
and there are no herds in the stalls,
yet I will celebrate in the LORD;
I will rejoice in the God of my salvation!
The LORD my Lord is my strength;
he makes my feet like those of a deer
and enables me to walk on mountain heights!
(vv. 17–19)

FIVE

Gideon's Weak Faith Made Strong

Gideon and the hundred men who were with him went to the outpost . . . They held their torches in their left hands and their rams' horns to blow in their right hands, and shouted, "A sword for the Lord *and for Gideon!"*
—Judges 7:19–20

You do not need great faith, but faith in a great God.
—James Hudson Taylor (1832–1905)

Over seventy years ago, I had a paper route handing out the *Ashland Daily Independent*. Each time I passed by, my friend John, who lived across the street from me, began shouting out with sarcasm and laughter, "R. T.'s dad's a Gideon, R. T.'s dad's a Gideon." I never thought my father being a Gideon would bring any kind of embarrassment or reproach for my beliefs. But John's teasing made an indelible impression on me. I knew about the Gideons—an international Christian association for men that exists largely to give out Bibles—but it did not cross my mind that fellow students in my neighborhood might make fun of them. What I have learned about the Gideons over the years is how many testimonies they have procured from people who were planning to take their lives but then reached into a hotel bedside table drawer and found a Gideon Bible. In reading it, both their lives and souls were saved in the nick of time. I often make the comment that I never knew a bad Gideon!

One could say that the Gideons' namesake in the Bible had low self-esteem. At a time when the people of Israel were undergoing great stress and their enemies—the Midianites—were stealing their crops, God himself appeared to hear their cry. When an angel of God came to Gideon and said, "The Lord is with you, valiant warrior," Gideon began to complain. First, he said, "If the Lord is with us, why has all this happened?"

God replied, "Go in the strength you have and deliver Israel from the grasp of Midian. I am sending you!"

Gideon continued to argue. "How can I deliver Israel? Look, my family is the weakest in Manasseh, and I am the youngest in my father's family."

"But I will be with you," the Lord said to Gideon. "You will strike Midian down as if it were one man" (Judg. 6:11–16).

In this chapter I want you to see a vital and important truth: the teaching of imputation. To impute means to "put to the credit of" or "to be charged with." God saw Gideon as a "valiant warrior," but Gideon did not feel that way! Nevertheless, God chose to see him differently than he saw himself. Indeed, blessed is the person to whom God does not impute sin (Rom. 4:8).

Although God looked on Gideon with great favor, Gideon's

faith was weak—very weak. So he asked for a sign, that is, proof, that God was truly speaking with him. The angel replied, "I will stay until you return" (Judg. 6:18).

Gideon prepared a young goat and unleavened bread for the angel, then placed the meat in a basket and the broth in a pot. The angel said to him, "Take the meat with the unleavened bread, put it on this stone, and pour the broth on it." Gideon did so. The angel touched the food with his staff, fire came up, and he vanished. Gideon got the sign; he realized that this mysterious figure was the angel of the Lord. Although Gideon feared imminent death, the angel granted peace to him by giving assurance that he would not die (vv. 19–23).

After that Gideon tore down an idol devoted to the worship of Baal. His faith was growing. Furthermore, as his faith increased, he blew the ram's horn and people began to follow him.

However, Gideon still needed more assurance. He said to God:

> If you will deliver Israel by me, as you said, I will put a wool fleece here on the threshing floor. If dew is only on the fleece, and all the ground is dry, I will know that you will deliver Israel by me, as you said. (vv. 36–37)

The day after asking for God's assurance, Gideon got up early and squeezed the fleece and wrung dew out of it, filling a bowl with water. God had answered his prayer.

But Gideon needed still more assurance! He then said to God:

> Don't be angry with me; let me speak one more time. Please allow me to make one more test with the fleece. Let it remain dry, and the dew be all over the ground. (v. 39)

That night God did yet again as Gideon requested: "only the fleece was dry, and dew was all over the ground" (v. 40).

So, God had twice answered Gideon exactly as Gideon requested. Are we to think that God was disgusted with Gideon?

In fact, this was the moment of Gideon's finest hour. He did not feel anything extraordinary happening, but God was at the bottom of it all. Remember that Jesus said, "Whoever is faithful in very little is also faithful in much" (Luke 16:10). Gideon was utterly humbled. He had no sense of entitlement. He was embarrassed to ask yet again for a similar sign. Having such weak faith was nothing to brag about. But this was a case of God accepting Gideon just as he was. Gideon would never—ever—be able to get glory for himself. He could only be thankful.

The fleece scenario prepared Gideon for the victory for which he became famous.

Reader, do you feel that your faith is weak? Be encouraged. If God could use Gideon, he can use you or me!

But the time came when Gideon did not test the Lord but this time the Lord tested Gideon. In Judges 7 God told Gideon that he had "too many troops." After Gideon dismissed those who were fearful, God ordered him to take the remaining men to the water and find out who would be selected to be in the forthcoming battle. God narrowed the number from an initial twenty-two thousand to three hundred! It turned out that those who lapped water with their hands like a dog rather than kneeling to drink were chosen (vv. 4–6). These men may have never discovered why they were chosen. Likewise, you and I may never find out why God has laid his hand on us. I can tell you this much: it was not because of our good works (2 Tim. 1:9)!

This is a timely reminder that you and I are not chosen for unusual ability or talent in ourselves. That we accidentally lap water with our hands, as it were, is why we are used of God! Jesus said to the disciples, "You did not choose me, but I chose you" (John 15:16). This should help us to not be so proud.

One of the best things to learn from the Gideon story as a whole is how patient God was with Gideon. He wants us simply to believe his word—not necessarily to have an extraordinary faith! Throughout the story Gideon remained weak. He needed more faith. God knew this. Did God lecture him? Did God moralize to Gideon and say, "Shame on you for not having great faith"? No. And just when Gideon needed more faith, God himself sent to Gideon exactly what he needed—more encouragement! God himself had already determined the victory for Gideon, and it was settled in God's eyes. Yes—in God's eyes and mind, it was done!

But God knew that Gideon was still worried, even after the episodes of the fleece and the choosing of the three hundred men. So the Lord said to Gideon, as it were, "I know how you can get a bit of encouragement. Do this, if you are afraid to attack just yet: 'Go down with Purah your servant' and eavesdrop on those Midianites. Just 'listen to what they say, and then you will be encouraged to attack the camp'" (cf. Judg. 7:10–11).

Gideon did exactly that. He heard a man telling his friend about a dream: "A loaf of barley bread came tumbling into the Midianite camp, struck a tent, and it fell. The loaf turned the tent upside down so that it collapsed." The friend replied, "This is nothing less than the sword of Gideon son of Joash, the Israelite. God has handed the entire Midianite camp over to him" (vv. 13–14).

When Gideon heard the account of the dream and its interpretation, he bowed in worship. He knew that the victory was a "slam dunk," as we might say today! With total confidence and full assurance, Gideon took full charge of his three hundred men: "Get up, for the LORD has handed the Midianite camp over to you." With ever-increasing confidence Gideon said, "Watch me and do what I do." First, they were to blow their rams' horns when Gideon did, saying, "For the LORD and for Gideon!" Then they were to break the pitchers that were in their hands. In other words, simultaneously blowing their horns and shattering their pitchers. They held their torches in their left hands, blowing horns in their right hands, and shouted "A sword for the LORD and for Gideon!" The entire Midianite army panicked, running and turning on each other with their swords (vv. 15–22). The victory indeed came soon!

Dear reader: God has a purpose for you. Your finest hour may be at hand. And the same tender, loving, and patient God that directed Gideon every step of the way offers to do the same thing for you.

Gideon had been faithful in the least. He proved to be faithful in much.

SIX

Elijah and Sharing the Glory

Elijah replied, "You have asked for something difficult. If you see me being taken from you, you will have it. If not, you won't."

—2 Kings 2:10

Few men have the natural strength to honor a friend's success without envy.

—Aeschylus (c. 525–c. 456 BC)

Elijah and Moses were the two greatest prophets in the Bible. They appeared with Jesus on the Mount of Transfiguration. Although Elijah gave his mantle plus a double portion of his spirit to Elisha, people did not talk about Elisha after he died. Rather, Elijah's name remained on their lips. The last verse in the Old Testament reminds us of the importance of Elijah:

> I am going to send you the prophet Elijah before the great and terrible day of the LORD comes. And he will turn the hearts of fathers to their children and the hearts of children to their fathers. Otherwise, I will come and strike the land with a curse. (Mal. 4:5–6)

Indeed, Elijah was so unusual and his miracles so extraordinary—especially the fire coming down from heaven to expose the hypocrisy of the false prophets—that the faithful of old and we may forget that he was an ordinary person—"a human being as we are" (James 5:17). There was no one like him.

Nevertheless, since Elijah was indeed a human being, it stands to reason that he would have had the same temptations and sorrows like us—such as sex, the lure of money, the potential for illnesses, and pride. We know that Elijah was a proud man who was also a bit uncaring. For example, on Mount Carmel in front of hundreds he said, "I am the only remaining prophet of the LORD" (1 Kings 18:22). That was not true—Elijah had been with Obadiah only a day or two before (v. 18:7ff). Even if we grant that this was an accidental omission, it shows how Elijah took himself more seriously than the other prophets. Furthermore, after Elijah performed powerfully if not spectacularly on Mount Carmel, he was terrified of being found by the wicked Jezebel soon after (19:1–5). He was very human, indeed.

My point in focusing on Elijah's humanity is this. Though he had no equal and no rival, he was very human—which is encouraging for us! That said, just before his departure Elijah did say to Elisha, "Tell me what I can do for you before I am taken from you" (2 Kings 2:9a). Elisha indeed had a request to make of his mentor: "Please let me inherit two shares of your spirit" (v. 9b; many versions call it a "double portion"). Whether Elijah expected this request or not, I don't know. But I don't think he was thrilled. One would have thought that the great Elijah would be delighted with Elisha's request. If I am honest with you, I think this got Elijah's goat—it made him upset. After all, Elijah discovered Elisha—a nobody—plowing with twelve teams of oxen. And now, not too long afterward, Elisha puts this bold request to the great Elijah! Was this a sign of Elisha's driving ambition—or was it actually evidence of his deep spirituality? Why would a person want a double portion? Why not wish merely for Elijah's mantle? Yes, that would have been a reasonable, unselfish request. But, instead, Elisha, a man who has come out of the blue, wants a *double portion* of the great Elijah's spirit.

Elijah's reply: "You have asked for something difficult" (v. 10). But why would this be so difficult? Is it difficult for God? God, after all, can do anything—at the snap of his finger. Was it difficult for the protégé Elisha? No, not at all—Elisha was eager. But, actually, it was difficult for Elijah.

Elijah had to have been aware that he was very unusual and famous. He had been used of God in an unprecedented way. No one since Moses—hundreds of years before—had been that famous, respected, or used of God Almighty. But there is more to keep in mind. Elijah had been preparing his ministry for over three years to expose and defeat the prophets of Baal and Asherah. Before this, we know virtually nothing about him, except that he was from Tishbe. But as soon as Elijah announced to King Ahab that there would not be a drop of rain—not even dew on the grass—until he himself gave the word (1 Kings 17:1), he had to go into hiding. For three years no one knew where

Elijah was. In the meantime, his own faith had been challenged during the drought while he trusted God to feed him through the ravens in the wilderness (vv. 2–5). After Elijah had to leave the wilderness, he met a poor widow who was preparing to die from starvation. He boldly asked her to feed him first (vv. 8–16)! Next, the widow's only son died, but God raised him to life through Elijah's prayers (vv. 17–24). In a word: Elijah's own faith had been tested to the hilt for those three years. And, now, after Elijah had been used by God in such unprecedented ways, his chosen successor Elisha wants Elijah to give him a double anointing in a couple of seconds!

Truthfully, it was not hard for God to do this. It was not hard for Elisha to receive the double portion. But I think it was hard for Elijah to grant this request. It is very rare for a man in his natural strength to honor another man's success without feeling envy. Elijah was human. It would have been absolutely normal and understandable for Elijah to hesitate to grant Elisha's request. After all, Elisha would get a double anointing without having labored for the Lord over the years. This anointing would give Elisha the stature of Elijah without working for it or having to wait for it. Given Elijah's fame and success, a double anointing would mean more miracles, more power, and more fame to the inexperienced Elisha. Yes—Elisha asked a difficult thing.

Thankfully, Elijah did not slap Elisha on the wrist for such a request. Indeed, the condition Elijah set was minimal. The only requirement was for Elisha to see Elijah ascend in a chariot of fire the same second he went up. No more. Elisha just needed to watch and not let his mind wander, be diverted, or look elsewhere—even for a second.

It seems that Elisha had a sort of premonition—or something

like that—all day before Elijah's departure. Whenever Elijah threatened to go anywhere, Elisha said in so many words, "You will not go without me" (2 Kings 2:1–6). Elisha was in Elijah's face sixty seconds a minute nonstop all day long. His instinct kept his eyes glued to the extraordinary prophet.

Elisha assumed that Elijah had the power to grant or withhold this request. Otherwise, Elisha would not have made such a weighty request, or Elijah would say, "It's not up to me." Elijah seemed to know that he was in some sense in charge of what followed.

> As they continued walking and talking, a chariot of fire with horses of fire suddenly appeared and separated the two of them. Then Elijah went up to heaven in the whirlwind. (v. 11)

Elisha's request was granted. He kept crying out, strangely, "My father, my father, the chariots and horsemen of Israel!" (v. 12).

This was Elijah's finest hour. He passed on the double anointing to his protégé.

All these things said, Elijah's mantle with a double portion of his spirit would never have happened without God—simple as that. I wonder if Elijah might have stopped it if it was entirely up to him. God—with Elijah's approval—granted this double portion to the unworthy, unprepared, inexperienced, and unknown Elisha. Elijah became willing to be surpassed in power, glory, and reputation by the man he chose to succeed him. Even though Elisha never outmatched Elijah's prominence in the end, that is not the point. The point is that Elijah was willing to give up his preeminence.

Elijah finished well in more ways than one.

SEVEN

Jeremiah and Being Falsely Accused

You are to say to them, "This is what the LORD says: If you do not listen to me by living according to my instruction that I set before you and by listening to the words of my servants the prophets—whom I have been sending to you time and time again, though you did not listen—I will make this temple like Shiloh. I will make this city an example for cursing for all the nations of the earth."

—Jeremiah 26:4–6

Then the priests and prophets said to the officials and all the people, "[Jeremiah] deserves the death sentence because he has prophesied against this city, as you have heard with your own ears."

—Jeremiah 26:11

Nobody has rightly denied himself unless he has wholly resigned himself to the Lord and is willing to leave every detail to his good pleasure. If we put ourselves in such a frame of mind, then, whatever may happen to us, we shall never feel miserable or accuse God falsely because of our lot.

—John Calvin (1509–1564)

The days following the 2020 presidential election in the US made me think a lot about Jeremiah, and perhaps more so about his contemporary Hananiah. Jeremiah prophesied during the reigns of Josiah, Jehoahaz, Jehoiakim, Jehoiachin, and Zedekiah—from roughly 626 BC to 587 BC. Jeremiah stood alone in his day and his prophecies were immensely unpopular. His unprecedented ministry was predicting the destruction of Jerusalem and the captivity of the people of Judah into Babylon.

"This will never happen!" retorted the people. The people of Judah knew they were chosen of God and that Jerusalem was the apple of God's eye. Nothing—ever—would cause Jerusalem to be destroyed or the people of God to be held captive by godless Babylon.

Jeremiah was consequently accused of treason. He was vilified, mistreated, and punished by multiple kings. He said what was unthinkable, namely, that Jerusalem would be like Shiloh, the place where the ark of the covenant had earlier dwelt (Jer. 7:12–15; 26:1–6). Because of the disobedience of the people, Shiloh became nothing: it was reduced to ruins. The people of Judah believed that Shiloh's fate would *never—ever*—happen to the hallowed Jerusalem. Thus, Jeremiah's prediction isolated him and he stood alone. However, the day indeed came that

Jerusalem was destroyed. King Zedekiah was blinded by the Babylonians and taken to Babylon.

As if that wasn't bad enough, a new issue emerged: How long would the captivity last?

In addition to the prophecy that Jerusalem would be destroyed and Judah would be taken captive to Babylon, Jeremiah also stood alone by maintaining that the Babylonian captivity would last seventy years.

Nobody in Judah wanted to hear such news.

Enter Hananiah. He prophesied news the people did want to hear, claiming to speak for God:

> This is what the Lord of Armies, the God of Israel, says: "I have broken the yoke of the king of Babylon. Within two years I will restore to this place all the articles of the Lord's temple that King Nebuchadnezzar of Babylon took from here and transported to Babylon. And I will restore to this place Jeconiah son of Jehoiakim, king of Judah, and all the exiles from Judah who went to Babylon"—this is the Lord's declaration—"for I will break the yoke of the king of Babylon." (28:2–4)

Hananiah claimed the captivity would last two years; Jeremiah said it would last seventy years.

Jeremiah had to wait a long time before he was vindicated regarding the seventy-year captivity of Judah. Hananiah's exposure, on the other hand, happened much sooner. Jeremiah did speak graciously to the prophet Hananiah in the presence of the priests and all the people who were standing in the temple of the Lord:

> Amen! May the LORD do that. May the LORD make the words you have prophesied come true and may he restore the articles of the LORD's temple and all the exiles from Babylon to this place! Only listen to this message I am speaking in your hearing and in the hearing of all the people. The prophets who preceded you and me from ancient times prophesied war, disaster, and plague against many lands and great kingdoms. As for the prophet who prophesies peace—only when the word of the prophet comes true will the prophet be recognized as one the LORD has truly sent. (vv. 6–9)

Perhaps Jeremiah wished that Hananiah was right and tried to spare him shame. Did Jeremiah seek to give Hananiah a chance to reject his lie? Or, sadly, did Hananiah's false prophecy have such a grip on him that he had to see it through?

But Hananiah impudently took the yoke bar that Jeremiah had been wearing as an object lesson about needing to submit to the Babylonians and broke it. Hananiah then proclaimed before all the people: "This is what the LORD says: 'In this way, within two years I will break the yoke of King Nebuchadnezzar of Babylon from the neck of all the nations'" (v. 11).

That ended any conciliatory thoughts Jeremiah might have had. Not long after this exchange, Jeremiah spoke God's word boldly and frankly to the prophet Hananiah: "Listen, Hananiah! The LORD did not send you, but you have led these people to trust in a lie. Therefore, this is what the LORD says, 'I am about to send you off the face of the earth. You will die this year because you have preached rebellion against the LORD'" (vv. 15–16). The prophet Hananiah indeed died in the seventh month of that year (v. 17).

Hananiah's obstinance reminds me of the twenty-first century charismatic prophets who tried to give millions of Christians a word they wanted to hear. These prophets stood together in predicting that Donald Trump would win a second term as US president in 2020. The majority of evangelical and charismatic Christians, overwhelmingly favoring Trump, wanted this outcome. But the prophecy failed. *The New York Times* actually wrote an article exposing the folly of these prophets. But did these prophets say, "Sorry—we got it wrong"? No. They stuck to their guns, believing that the Democrats had stolen the election from Trump. Interestingly, I know of one man, Jeremiah Johnson (another Jeremiah!), who humbled himself and apologized for prophesying falsely. Many in our day thus turned against this Jeremiah. Both Jeremiahs were alone in their responses to the truth.

I understand why Jeremiah is referred to as "the weeping prophet." The nature of his prophecies and the way his ministry was rejected by virtually all Israel gave him a depressing life.

Imagine you were called to speak or lead, and no one believed you or wanted to follow your directions.

Jeremiah, having been chosen from his mother's womb, was raised up to prophesy what people did not want to hear. What a calling! What a future! He was not what one might term a "roaring success." He preached God's word for some fifty years and was never popular. But he pleased God. We all might want to be in Jeremiah's shoes at the judgment. God is still looking for those who are willing to be Jeremiahs on this earth.

The Israelites misunderstood what it meant to be chosen of God and believed that Jerusalem was perpetually God's favorite spot on earth. They took it for granted that their future was secure and safe and that nobody could succeed against them. But Moses had warned that the future of Israel was based upon obedience to God's law. Jeremiah faithfully carried out Moses's warning, but no one wanted to hear his words.

And that was Jeremiah's finest hour—when he stood alone and stayed faithful to his mission.

How much would you be willing to endure or lose, as Jeremiah did, to speak the truth about God's ways?

EIGHT

Jephthah and the World's Opposition

This is what Jephthah says: "Israel did not take away the land of Moab or the land of the Ammonites. But when they came from Egypt, Israel traveled through the wilderness to the Red Sea and came to Kadesh . . . While Israel lived three hundred years in Heshbon and Aroer and their surrounding villages, and in all the cities that are on the banks of the Arnon, why didn't you take them back at that time? I have not sinned against you, but you are doing me wrong by fighting against me. Let the Lord who is the judge decide today between the Israelites and the Ammonites" . . . Jephthah crossed over to the Ammonites to fight against them, and the Lord handed them over to him.

—Judges 11:15–16; 26–27; 32

What more can I say? Time is too short for me to tell about . . . Jephthah.

—Hebrews 11:32

Their Finest Hour

Let us, then, go to him outside the camp, bearing his disgrace.
—Hebrews 13:13

If the world is against Athanasius, Athanasius is against the world.
—Athanasius (c. 296–373)

Jephthah is probably the least-known person in Hebrews 11. Jephthah's infamous vow regarding his daughter, his only child, in Judges 11 is probably why people remember him. Indeed, most of us would never—ever—have thought of Jephthah as warranting a place in Hebrews 11! Fortunately, the writer of Hebrews sees people as God does—not as man does.

Several interesting issues emerge in the life of Jephthah. First, he was not "mainstream." Whatever is mainstream? It is hard to argue with Scripture that he shouldn't have been a judge. But Jephthah's family origin didn't make him the ideal candidate to lead God's people. He was the son of a prostitute (Judg. 11:1), which puts him outside of the mainstream. Many of us fancy that *we* are in the mainstream. We are tempted to view ourselves or our churches as God's mainstream. Perhaps our church movement has reasons to praise God for using it in the past. But that is no guarantee for how God will use it now.

The second thing that emerges in Jephthah's life deals with the likelihood of being greatly used of God. The manifestly obvious thing about Jephthah was that he was not likely at all to be sought after as a leader. His half-brothers (Gilead, Jephthah's father, had a wife and legitimate children with her) forced him to leave the house of his father. But the truth is, Jephthah was a born leader! When God looks for the next person to be used, he bypasses aspects that may well put people off.

Worst of all: Jephthah attracted the scum of the earth. The nobodies of this world followed Jephthah. My Bible refers to the people who followed him as "worthless men" (v. 3). Other than these fringe characters, all Israel was against Jephthah. He was grossly unattractive to the mainstream of Israel.

And yet the time came when Israel was in deep, deep trouble. Their situation was so serious that they were prepared to overlook traditional ways of thinking and the notions of the majority. They then saw in Jephthah a leadership gift. Indeed, he was an intellectual genius. The rank and file of the Israelites decided to go "outside the camp" and go to Jephthah on bended knee for help.

Are you outside the camp? If so, this is a good place to be. You may not be in the social mainstream, but in God's eyes those outside the camp may be in the mainstream! Often God turns to those outside the camp when he wants to begin a new work. Everybody knew about Jephthah, but no people that "mattered" called on him until one day they turned to him in desperation.

Are you wondering why Hebrews 11 mentions Jephthah? What was his faith? Judges 11 shows us that Jephthah had a brilliant understanding of God's purpose in history. He may have been rejected and an outcast in Israel, but he knew his history. He put his enemies to shame by his knowledge of theology and history.

Let me describe the situation. The king of the Ammonites accused Israel of stealing his people's land, an event that had taken place three hundred years before. Jephthah knew better and point by point traced every step of the children of Israel from the time they left Egypt through their time in the wilderness. He revealed that God had dispossessed the Ammonites, telling their king: "We have been around for three hundred years; why are you getting anxious all of a sudden?" In a way Jephthah won the intellectual argument, but his words did not impress the Ammonites. Jephthah's finest hour came about when he could no longer depend on his own knowledge. He dropped the intellectual argument and turned everything over to God! Jephthah's trust in the Lord was strong, and he asked God to settle the whole matter (Judg. 11:27). And God indeed settled the matter! God stepped in and handed the Ammonites over to Israel.

Many who have giant intellects imagine that God will use their ability to reason and present convincing arguments. Perhaps he does. But Jephthah, someone capable of reasoning and fighting, experienced his finest hour when he simply put his faith in God to settle the matter.

Unfortunately, Jephthah is mostly remembered for his rash vow. He made a huge error; he thought he needed to impress God by making a vow. As he went out to confront the Ammonites in battle, Jephthah vowed that he would sacrifice as a burnt offering the first person to greet him upon his return home if God would give him the victory. God gave him the victory, but the first person he met after coming home was his own beloved daughter! As far as we know, he kept his vow (vv. 29–40). Sadly, the best of God's people still have blemishes in their lives. As John Calvin once said, "In every saint there is something reprehensible."

Jephthah's memory is blemished. He had a finest hour, but he also made a vow that resulted in real harm. Ultimately, he did earn a place in Hebrews 11. To me that shows that God remembers Jephthah differently than how the rest of us remember him.

NINE

Sarah's No Joke Laugh

"Where is your wife Sarah?" they asked him.

"There, in the tent," he answered.

The Lord *said, "I will certainly come back to you in about a year's time, and your wife Sarah will have a son!" Now Sarah was listening at the entrance of the tent behind him.*

Abraham and Sarah were old and getting on in years. Sarah had passed the age of childbearing. So she laughed to herself: "After I am worn out and my lord is old, will I have delight?"

But the Lord *asked Abraham, "Why did Sarah laugh, saying, 'Can I really have a baby when I'm old?' Is anything impossible for the* Lord*? At the appointed time I will come back to you, and in about a year she will have a son."*

Sarah denied it. "I did not laugh," she said, because she was afraid.

But he replied, "No, you did laugh."

—Genesis 18:9–15

Their Finest Hour

By faith even Sarah herself, when she was unable to have children, received power to conceive offspring, even though she was past the age, since she considered that the one who had promised was faithful.

—Hebrews 11:11

He who laughs last, laughs best.

—John Heywood, *Book of Proverbs* (1546)

I want to draw your attention to two similar phrases in the New Testament: "receive power" and "received power." Jesus said that the disciples would "receive power" when the Holy Spirit would come upon them (Acts 1:8). And the writer of Hebrews said that Sarah "received power" to conceive the baby Isaac although she was ninety years old. The Greek word for power in both places is *dunamis*.

The emergence of the supernatural in the Old Testament is most prominent in the book of Exodus. In Exodus 3:2–6, God showed up in the burning bush. Following that remarkable sight came the ten plagues on Pharaoh, the crossing of the Red Sea, the manna in the desert, and other instances during the Israelites' forty years in the wilderness.

That said, the birth of Isaac in the book of Genesis was totally miraculous. Sarah received "power" by faith to have a baby at the age of ninety—long after she had stopped menstruating. This work of the Holy Spirit was every bit as powerful as the Spirit of God coming down in Moses's day or the flames of fire descending on the early church at Pentecost.

Over forty years ago I drove Dr. Martyn Lloyd-Jones to the Cotswolds in England, where he preached annually. While we were eating in a restaurant on the way, I asked him to give me a good definition of *faith*. It was the late summer of 1979; I was planning to begin a series of sermons on Hebrews 11 in Westminster Chapel. Dr. Lloyd-Jones smiled, almost chuckled, and said, "I only know one other person who thinks like you," adding, "I would never think of coming up with a definition of faith."

I replied, "But I am still asking you; give me a good definition of faith!"

Dr. Lloyd-Jones couldn't think of any at that time. But the next morning the phone rang. The familiar voice on the other end of the line said: "*Believing God*. There's your definition." He then quoted Scripture after Scripture from the KJV, including verses like: "[Abraham] believed in the LORD" (Gen. 15:6) and "I believe God" (Acts 27:25), spoken by Paul on the ship to Malta. Dr. Lloyd-Jones then said: "I can't wait to preach this myself." I have used that definition of faith in my sermons covering Hebrews 11 ever since.

"Believing God," in my opinion, is truly an unimprovable definition of faith. Hebrews 11:1 is, of course, a kind of definition of faith: "Faith is the reality of what is hoped for, the proof of what is not seen." But Hebrews 11:1 clarifies or describes what makes faith *faith*. It asserts that faith is not based on evidence but on belief in the heart without empirical proof. Dr. Lloyd-Jones's definition presupposes that God is the object of faith. God has spoken, and you believe him. You believe what he said, what he promised, and what he predicted. Faith means *believing God's word*.

When Sarah overheard the word from the angel to Abraham, she knew in her heart that it was a word from God.

And, yes, she laughed. Yes, it was a cynical laugh. Yes, she was afraid. But the truth is: Sarah knew it was a no-joke word. *She believed God.*

Have you ever had a nervous laugh that rolled out because the news seemed too good to be true? I suspect that Sarah's laughter had that dynamic. Her laughter contained mixed feelings. She had faith and unbelief at the same time. Could she be happy and afraid simultaneously? The disciples of Jesus, after all, had "fear and great joy" on Easter Sunday (Matt. 28:8). Having a baby at the age of ninety was a lot to take in.

But the Lord also said to Abraham, "Why did Sarah laugh, saying, 'Can I really have a baby when I'm old?'" This word of the Lord, which Sarah also heard, showed that God understood the unusual nature of such a prophecy. That is why a word of tenderness and understanding accompanied the promise: "Is anything impossible for the Lord?" (Gen. 18:13–14). By the way, Sarah's laugh was to herself—what she did was private! But it shows that God sees our thoughts. Sarah denied laughing to Abraham. But God knew she had laughed—not out loud, but to herself. I think we could speculate for ages about the explanation of Sarah's laughter. I suspect it was a mixture of fear and joy, cynicism and excitement, and doubt and belief.

Thankfully, we know this: faith won. "By faith even Sarah . . . received power to conceive." She believed God, and God stepped in. He who gave the promise supplied the power to enable her to conceive.

But there is more. Sarah could see that God was giving her a second chance. After experiencing barrenness her whole life, the news that she would have a baby boy seemed too good to be true.

The God of the Bible is the God of the second chance! You may be absolutely sure that Sarah had lived for some fifteen years with a deep, deep regret. She really regretted giving Abraham bad advice about Hagar—which he had taken. Sarah knew that her husband was discouraged that the initial promise to him that he would have a son (15:5)—he was eighty-five and she seventy-five—was seemingly not being fulfilled. Perhaps she felt guilty about her barrenness and blamed herself. But she wanted to help make good the promise—which she apparently also believed. So Sarah said, "the Lord has prevented me from bearing children" (16:2). She reasoned that the Lord could give her children by Hagar, her Egyptian servant. Abraham and Sarah both apparently felt they needed to help God make good on his promise. Abraham took her advice; Hagar became his wife, Abraham assuming that this was the way the birth of a male child was supposed to happen. And it did happen—Hagar conceived a child.

But when Hagar became pregnant, things went wrong—Sarah and Hagar fell out with each other. Sarah looked with contempt upon Hagar, and also began to blame Abraham for everything. Hagar likewise began to show contempt toward Sarah. Abraham, possibly feeling some guilt, gave Sarah permission to do as she wished toward Hagar. She did, and Hagar fled this mistreatment. But while Hagar was running from Sarah, lo and behold, the angel of the Lord appeared to her. The Lord told Hagar to return to Sarah and instructed her to give the child the name Ishmael (vv. 4–16).

Abraham assumed for thirteen years that Ishmael was the promised child that God had in mind when he initially gave the promise in Genesis 15:5. I can't prove this, but I suspect that Sarah felt no fondness toward Ishmael—or Hagar—for those thirteen years. I think Abraham did love Ishmael. In any case, God had a plan for Ishmael's seed. God said that he would multiply Ishmael greatly, making him into a great nation (17:20).

The thought to Sarah that she would have a baby—indeed, the promised son that was meant in Genesis 15:5—inspired her to continue holding on to the promise. Yes, she "considered that the one who had promised was faithful" (Heb. 11:11). So, at age ninety, Sarah was given a second chance. This time she was determined not to blow it. She believed God and would not give up—despite her age and despite the fact that nothing like this had ever happened before. Mind you, Sarah had Abraham with her all the way. He, too, was challenged. He did not falter in faith when he considered the weakness of his own body—"already dead"—or when he considered "the deadness of Sarah's womb." Rather, Abraham was "fully convinced that what God had promised, he was also able to do" (Rom. 4:19–21).

When Sarah laughed at God's news, this was actually her finest hour. We don't know if any other people laughed when they heard the news that a ninety-year-old woman was expecting a baby—and that she knew it would be a son. But we know that Sarah herself laughed at the thought. And her laugh was the last laugh. For thousands of years the people of God would salute her.

Sarah also set the standard of how a person can make a big mistake and be forgiven. And she was not only forgiven but was also exalted as an example of how God can take our mistakes and cause all things to work together for good.

TEN

Rahab and Seizing the Wave of the Future

By faith Rahab the prostitute welcomed the spies in peace and didn't perish with those who disobeyed.
—Hebrews 11:31

It is great to be faced with the impossible, for nothing is impossible if one is meant to do it. Wisdom will be given, and strength. When the Lord leads, He always strengthens.
—Amy Carmichael (1867–1951)

Rahab was a prostitute who lived in the walled city of Jericho. We don't know anything about Rahab's relationship with the true God or how much she knew prior to her encounter with God's people. She likely knew something of God's reputation. The word had spread all over Canaan about the Israelites crossing the Red Sea forty years before. The people of Jericho would also have known about the Israelites' recent crossing of the Jordan River into Canaan—only a few miles away from their city. Terror likely struck all of the people of Jericho and the surrounding territories as they realized that the Israelites were determined to conquer Canaan. The citizens of Jericho likely expected that they would be attacked first.

Joshua dispatched two spies to investigate the city of Jericho (Josh. 2). You may recall that Moses had sent twelve spies into Canaan many years before to check it out. But the majority voted ten to two not to go into the land at that time, even though this land was theirs by God's promise. So, Israel could have been in Canaan thirty-eight years before—but unbelief prevailed and all of the children of Israel died in the wilderness except for Joshua and Caleb.

Now, it was time to try again. Recall that Joshua had experienced the awe of God when encountering the commander of the army of the Lord. Having envisaged Jericho as being the first major city of Canaan to be conquered, Joshua awaited a word from the two spies before taking any action.

The two spies visited the house of Rahab. It is not known if they knew she was a prostitute. Maybe they thought that Rahab would more likely welcome visitors than other residents who might be afraid to let strangers in. The text doesn't say whether their knocking on Rahab's door was on purpose or by chance. In any case, it was in God's plan.

Rahab could not believe her luck when these two Israelite spies knocked on her door! She knew exactly who they were as well as what she should do for them. Rahab knew that her future and security were in their hands since the reputation of the children of Israel had spread all over the known world. As I said earlier, everybody knew of the awesome and mighty things

God had done to deliver his people out of Egypt. He had also taken care of them in the wilderness despite their less-than-praiseworthy fidelity to him. And God had already inflicted judgment upon Sihon and Og by the hand of his people. All these events gave the Lord a reputation of being a God of glory and power.

In the meantime, the king of Jericho learned that two men from the children of Israel had come to search out the land and had entered Rahab's house. The king investigated Rahab and no doubt planned to arrest the men. But Rahab had a plan. She not only knew who the men were; she knew that the king would be knocking on her door to apprehend the spies.

She lied to the king, saying to him:

> Yes, the men did come to me, but I didn't know where they were from. At nightfall, when the city gate was about to close, the men went out, and I don't know where they were going. Chase after them quickly, and you can catch up with them! (vv. 4–5)

This was Rahab's finest hour.

The truth was, Rahab had quickly hid the spies. She brought them up to the roof and hid them with the stalks of flax that she had laid on there. These men were possibly very surprised and must have wondered why Rahab did this. The answer is that *she saw the wave of the future*. Rahab knew that Jericho would be conquered and that time was on Israel's side. She knew there was only one hope for her—that these spies might remember her and show kindness to her. After she lied to the king, she said these words to the two spies:

> I know that the Lord has given you this land and that the terror of you has fallen on us, and everyone who lives in the land is panicking because of you. For we have heard how the Lord dried up the water of the Red Sea before you when you came out of Egypt, and what you did to Sihon and Og, the two Amorite kings you completely destroyed across the Jordan. When we heard this, we lost heart, and everyone's courage failed because of you, for the Lord your God is God in heaven above and on earth below. Now please swear to me by the Lord that you will also show kindness to my father's family, because I showed kindness to you. Give me a sure sign that you will spare the lives of my father, mother, brothers, sisters, and all who belong to them, and save us from death. (vv. 9–13)

Hebrews 11:31 says Rahab did this "by faith." But if faith is "believing God," where had she heard God speak? The answer is: she believed the testimony about the success and the extraordinary survival of the Israelites from their time in Egypt until that moment! Moreover, the recent crossing of the Jordan River showed that the same God was with this new generation of Israelites. Rahab was being honest in her heart; she actually believed this in her own heart of hearts. The God of power and glory was taking over. The children of Israel were the wave of the future.

But note: those who perished with the fall of Jericho had "disobeyed" (v. 31). Rahab believed God; the inhabitants of Jericho disobeyed God.

One might accuse Rahab of being unpatriotic. In a sense, she stood alone against her people and their gods. She chose honesty over patriotism, and truth about the future over relationships. Our moment to stand alone will also come. We, too, need to be ready to stand before the judgment seat of Christ (2 Cor. 5:10). It is a future event, and there we will stand alone.

To put it another way, Rahab refused to live in denial as the people of Jesus's day would do later. The Pharisees and Sadducees could not deny that both Jesus and the apostles worked miracles (John 11:45–46; Acts 4:16). But they chose to live in denial rather than follow the truth. Rahab, on the other hand, refused to suppress the truth. She believed the God who spoke clearly by showing his power through the supernatural.

Rahab's honesty might also be contrasted with the people Paul described in Romans who chose to live in denial rather than accept the truth of God clearly revealed in nature (Rom. 1:18–28). Likewise, David wrote: "The heavens declare the glory of God, and the expanse proclaims the work of his hands" (Ps. 19:1). Sadly, people continue rejecting the truth even though nature and their consciences testify to that truth, and all too often many of them are turned over to a mind void of judgment, as Paul soberly explains.

These things said, since Rahab revealed what everybody was thinking, I would have thought that the king of Jericho could run with haste to Joshua and surrender! But, instead, Jericho would be foolishly, tightly locked. Indeed, Jericho was "strongly fortified because of the Israelites—no one leaving or entering" (Josh. 6:1).

Rahab made a deal with the two Israeli spies. In so many words, she asked that since she had dealt kindly with them, would they deal kindly with not just her, but also her family? Believing that an oath they swore by the Lord God of Israel would be absolutely kept, she made this proposition: "Give me a sure sign" that they would save her and her family when the Israelites invaded Jericho. "Swear to me by the LORD" was at the bottom of the deal she wanted to make with them. The men agreed and said to her, "We will give our lives for yours!" They did want a further word from her, that she would not "report our mission." In return, "we will show kindness and faithfulness to you when the LORD gives us the land" (2:12–14).

Rahab let the two spies down by a rope through the window. She told them where to go—"to the hill country"—then afterward to go on their way. The following exchange then occurred:

> The men said to her, ". . . when we enter the land, you tie this scarlet cord to the window through which you let us down. Bring your father, mother, brothers, and all your father's family into your house. If anyone goes out the doors of your house, his death will be his own fault, and we will be innocent. But if anyone with you in the house should be harmed, his death will be our fault. And if you report our mission, we are free from the oath you made us swear."
>
> "Let it be as you say," she replied, and she sent them away. After they had gone, she tied the scarlet cord to the window. (vv. 17–21)

You may be wondering how Rahab's lie could be her finest hour. Yes, it is fair to ask how lying could lead to something good. I certainly do not recommend that you practice lying. You will not get a finest hour by misleading people—that is not the takeaway from this chapter or book. Rather, I want you to consider what Rahab put her faith and trust in. She believed a message about an unfamiliar God who could deliver her and her family, a God she knew only through secondhand stories—rumors, if you will.

The word from the two spies to Joshua gave great encouragement! "The LORD has handed over the entire land to us. Everyone who lives in the land is also panicking because of us" (v. 24).

When the day of the fall of Jericho came, I can picture Rahab having another look at the scarlet rope—to be sure it was visible and in place. Her faith was no doubt challenged. She took a big risk in trusting the Israelites. The shouts of the Israelites would be heard from all over Jericho. "Will they remember?" she might have asked. Hebrews 11:31 says that Rahab's life was spared "by faith"—believing God. Joshua gave specific orders to the two spies once all the walls fell: "Go to the prostitute's house and bring the woman out of there, and all who are with her, just as you swore to her" (Josh. 6:22). Whether there was a knock on the door—or if they broke it down—I can only imagine. But the spies could have said something like this to Rahab: "Welcome sister, come with us."

Framing Rahab as a prostitute, as Scripture does, suggests that she would normally be a person to avoid. But Rahab had great faith—greater than others with more acceptable professions. It wasn't her work or reputation that saved her or helped Israel. Her faith in God saved her, and that testimony is what is retold over and over again.

You and I are identified with and have fellowship with a huge minority, namely, true, unashamed followers of Jesus Christ. Thus, we are probably disdained and laughed at more than ever, because our detractors can't see the heart of faith behind the questionable exterior.

Rahab discerned the wave of the future and became a legend.

ELEVEN

Deborah and Barak Relinquishing the Glory

Deborah, a prophetess and the wife of Lappidoth, was judging Israel at that time. She would sit under the palm tree of Deborah between Ramah and Bethel in the hill country of Ephraim, and the Israelites went up to her to settle disputes.

She summoned Barak son of Abinoam from Kedesh in Naphtali and said to him, "Hasn't the Lord*, the God of Israel, commanded you, 'Go, deploy the troops on Mount Tabor, and take with you ten thousand men from the Naphtalites and Zebulunites? Then I will lure Sisera commander of Jabin's army, his chariots, and his infantry at the Wadi Kishon to fight against you, and I will hand him over to you.'"*

Barak said to her, "If you will go with me, I will go. But if you will not go with me, I will not go."

"I will gladly go with you," she said, "but you will receive no honor on the road you are about to take, because the Lord *will sell Sisera to a woman."*

—Judges 4:4–9

Deborah and Barak Relinquishing the Glory

God wants us to have soft hearts and hard feet. The trouble with so many of us is that we have hard hearts and soft feet.

—Jackie Pullinger

It was my third year at Westminster Chapel and I was preaching through Hebrews 11. The week before I came to verse 32, the part which mentions Barak, I mentioned to Lady Elizabeth Catherwood (daughter of Dr. Martyn Lloyd-Jones), "I am working on a sermon on Barak for next Sunday." She replied, "I've always thought that Old Testament story is more about Deborah than Barak."

Elizabeth's remark got me thinking. I racked my brain that week to figure out why the writer of Hebrews mentioned Barak—and not Deborah—in the list of those valiant people whose faith led them to do extraordinary things.

For three hundred years following the era of Joshua, for some reason, no truly great leader rose—only people who are called "judges." An oddity of Israelite redemptive history is how God would raise up unusual leaders and successors, but then apparently raise up no one. For example, God raised up Moses, then Joshua. But after Joshua, he apparently raised up nobody.

Judges were selected to arbitrate in the affairs of Israel (i.e., civil or domestic quarrels) and to provide military leadership against impending enemies. Only a handful of these judges have much stature in Old Testament history. At that time the twelve tribes of Israel were each independent under a confederacy in the land of Canaan. But they had failed to wipe out all of the Canaanites, and the remaining Canaanites proved to be their constant enemy, causing endless troubles. More alarmingly, the Israelites had forgotten God. They began to make themselves at home in Canaan without remembering *who* had given them their land. They began to live as though nature was all there was. Finally, they ceased to be offended by strange gods in the land and were themselves soon driven to idolatry. However, Deborah was an exception.

Deborah was a godly woman, a prophetess, and the only female judge mentioned in the Bible. She was undoubtedly recognized as a prophet of God, being known as a "mother in Israel" (Judg. 5:7). There is no lead up to Deborah being appointed as a judge; Scripture simply names her, mentions her husband's name, and notes that she judged Israel at that time (4:4). The fact that a woman led Israel during this patriarchal period is interesting. It plays a role in the overlap of Deborah's and Barak's finest hours.

In her role as judge, Deborah appointed Barak as the Israelite general. God commanded him through Deborah to lead an attack upon the forces of Jabin, the king of Canaan. Sisera was Jabin's military commander. He had nine hundred iron chariots: a formidable type of weaponry and means of transportation. Barak agreed to lead the attack, but only if Deborah would go with him. Perhaps this portrays him as a weak leader. He believed Deborah's word, but he still needed her at his side.

Deborah agreed to go with Barak into battle, but warned him—being mindful of the male ego!—that he would forfeit any glory, a woman obtaining it instead.

Barak appears to have grasped all the implications and was determined only to go with Deborah at his side. They achieved a marvelous victory together. It was as though Barak would not move an inch without her prompting him. At the appropriate time, Deborah said, "Go! This is the day the Lord has handed

Sisera over to you. Hasn't the LORD gone before you?" The Lord routed Sisera and all his chariots and all his army before Barak. All of the army of Sisera "fell by the sword; not a single man was left" (vv. 14–16).

The story of strong and inspired women does not end there. Commander Sisera ran off from the battlefield on foot to the tent of Jael, the wife of Heber the Kenite, because there was peace between Jabin and the house of Heber. Jael welcomed Sisera and treated him with friendliness and kindness. She covered him with a blanket. He asked for water, so she opened a skin of milk and gave him a drink. He asked her to protect him and keep anybody from knowing he was there. But Jael quietly and secretly found a tent peg and a hammer. She went "silently" to Sisera and drove the peg into his temple while he was asleep. He died. This ended the battle (vv. 17–22). "The land had peace for forty years" (5:31).

Deborah the prophetess knew by the Holy Spirit that a woman—Jael—would get the glory. Did she also know that Barak would later be remembered for these events?

This brings me back to my question from the beginning of this chapter: Why does the writer of Hebrews mention Barak but not Deborah or Jael? Barak was indeed the general in charge and got the credit for winning the war. But his success came about because of Deborah.

I believe there are three reasons why Barak gets mentioned rather than Deborah. First, he was willing to appear weak. He did not impute to himself more faith than he had. He did not repeat the "Peter principle," that is, promoting himself to the level of his incompetence. He lived within the "measure" (limit) of his faith (Rom. 12:3). Second, he trusted Deborah's prophetic gift.

Barak knew that she heard from God minute by minute. He did not trust his military prowess without her leading all the way. Third, he was not seeking glory for himself in the first place, but was willing to let a woman have the glory. His humility, therefore, earned him a place in Hebrews 11. Affirming Deborah's leadership was his finest hour.

Deborah is to be saluted for warning Barak that a woman would go down in history as achieving the victory. But was that woman Deborah? Don't forget Jael! Judges 5 contains the song of Deborah and Barak—and Jael leaps out of the blue:

> In the days of Shamgar son of Anath,
> in the days of Jael,
> the main roads were deserted
> because travelers kept to the side roads. (v. 6)

> Most blessed of women is Jael,
> the wife of Heber the Kenite;
> she is most blessed among tent-dwelling women.
> He asked for water; she gave him milk.
> She brought him cream in a majestic bowl.
> She reached for a tent peg,
> her right hand, for a workman's hammer.
> Then she hammered Sisera—
> she crushed his head;
> she shattered and pierced his temple.
> He collapsed, he fell, he lay down between her feet;
> he collapsed, he fell between her feet;
> where he collapsed, there he fell—dead.
> (vv. 24–27)

Barak relinquished the glory. Deborah did try to get Barak to take the glory that would have been his—and yet she gets glory by trying to avoid getting glory! As if the humility of Deborah and Barak wasn't enough, the song of Deborah and Barak ends up exalting the hitherto unknown woman—Jael.

You might be tempted to think of Deborah as a feminist. Think again. Both Deborah and Barak are similar: Deborah wants Barak to get victory and receive glory, yet Barak is humble enough to know that Deborah had a special anointing without which there would be no victory. In both cases they were self-effacing. And the rise of Jael, a woman and an outsider, who receives more glory in the Judges narrative than Barak and Deborah, shows us that Deborah's and Barak's finest hours met at the same time. They were willing for their fame to go to the other person and, ultimately, to God alone.

Let me add a personal note. One Sunday evening at Westminster Chapel, I invited Jackie Pullinger to speak. Her reputation of leading thousands of drug addicts to the Lord Jesus Christ in Hong Kong speaks for itself. What inspired me to give her the pulpit—the first woman to speak there in Chapel history—was Deborah. Deborah was an exceptional woman. God had raised her up for her people in such a difficult time in Israelite history. Appealing to this event in the book of Judges, knowing how God has used Jackie in Hong Kong—which I witnessed for myself—I regard Jackie as a modern-day Deborah. The city of Hong Kong gave her vast property, on which she helps drug addicts recover. She does what hospitals fail to do. Jackie was ultimately given the Order of the British Empire medal by Queen Elizabeth II. Barak was not worried about his reputation, seeing God's hand clearly work through Deborah. Why should I be, either?

TWELVE

Esther and Mordecai Facing Death with Fearlessness

The entire royal staff at the King's Gate bowed down and paid homage to Haman, because the king had commanded this to be done for him. But Mordecai would not bow down or pay homage.

—Esther 3:2

I will go to the king even if it is against the law. If I perish, I perish.

—Esther 4:16

Never be afraid to trust an unknown future to a known God.

—Corrie ten Boom (1892–1983)

In the summer of 1975 my family and I traveled to Haarlem in the Netherlands. While there, I was privileged to meet a living legend, Corrie ten Boom. I asked her to pray for me.

"Why do you want me to pray for you?" she bluntly replied.

I told Corrie that I was working on a doctorate at Oxford University and that I felt ill-equipped, fearing I would fail.

She abruptly interrupted me in mid-sentence and blurted out, "Heavenly Father, show this man he does not need the prayers of Corrie ten Boom but only the prayers of the Lord Jesus Christ."

Whew! I was quickly put in my place, although Corrie kindly continued praying for me. Many readers will know that she helped her family protect Jews from the Nazis in World War II by hiding them in a small room above her father's jewelry store. I felt it was appropriate to quote Corrie at the beginning of this chapter because Queen Esther and Mordecai likewise courageously saved many Jews in ancient Susa, Persia (modern Iran).

I have followed the Bible reading plan designed by Robert Murray M'Cheyne for more than forty years. Each year when I come to Esther 3 and read about how Mordecai stubbornly and seemingly senselessly refused to pay homage to Haman, I cringe. I ask myself, "Why does Mordecai do this?" Showing courtesy and respect for a man whom the king of Persia wants to honor is surely a harmless thing to do. But when I get over my feeling of nervous awe, I look again at Mordecai's action. Rightly or wrongly, I then say to myself, "This shows the most courage and fearlessness of anybody in the Old Testament." Mordecai must have known how stupid he looked! But I still keep thinking that it would surely be harmless to show a little respect to a friend of the king! I doubt that any single human being who observed Mordecai's passive resistance felt any respect or admiration toward him.

You might be wondering, was this Mordecai's finest hour? Maybe—but let's look a bit more at how the book of Esther unfolds.

Just as we saw that women received the credit for the victory in our previous chapter with Deborah and Barak, Esther gets this biblical book named after her. But surely Mordecai's heroics should not be ignored! It turns out that Esther's courage is equal to Mordecai's. Esther and Mordecai needed each other, just like Deborah and Barak did.

Esther had lost her parents and was raised by Mordecai, a close relative. Through bizarre circumstances, the king of Persia rejected his queen Vashti and chose the beautiful and wise Esther to replace her (2:5–18). Mordecai advised Esther not to let it be known that she was Jewish (v. 10). In the meantime, Mordecai discovered a plot to assassinate the king and revealed it to Esther, saving the king's life (vv. 21–23). But Mordecai's loyalty apparently went unnoticed by the king. During this time Haman was promoted to be the most important person in Susa next to the king. Haman was a descendant of King Agag of the Amalekites, who were ancestral enemies of Israel (cf. 3:1; 1 Sam. 15), and so Mordecai refused to bow to him. Mordecai's snub so annoyed Haman—he was "filled with rage" (3:5)—that he decided to destroy all Jews in Persia. Haman persuaded the king to sign a document that guaranteed the destruction of all Jews, and then they celebrated together (v. 15).

Word reached Mordecai that Haman had managed to get the king to order the extermination of the Jews. Mordecai then did another strange thing that seemed ridiculous:

> [Mordecai] tore his clothes, put on sackcloth and ashes, went into the middle of the city, and cried loudly and bitterly. He went only as far as the King's Gate, since the law prohibited anyone wearing sackcloth from entering the King's Gate. (4:1–2)

This crying and noisy lamenting embarrassed Queen Esther. She was "overcome with fear" when she heard the news of her beloved Mordecai carrying on like this. She sent garments to clothe him, but he would not accept them. Esther then sent one of the king's eunuchs to find out what was going on. Mordecai gave the eunuch a copy of the written decree for the Jews' destruction and asked him to show it to Esther. Mordecai then asked Esther to beg the king's favor. However, Esther explained to Mordecai that anyone going to the king without being called would be put to death. Mercy would only be shown if the king held out the golden scepter. Esther had not been called to come to the king for thirty days (v. 11), so he would likely not be receptive to her presence or plea.

Mordecai then sent the following reply to Esther:

> Don't think that you will escape the fate of all the Jews because you are in the king's palace. If you keep silent at this time, relief and deliverance will come to the Jewish people from another place, but you and your father's family will be destroyed. Who knows, perhaps you have come to your royal position for such a time as this. (vv. 13–14)

I want to mention two things about the book of Esther. First, it is the only book in the Bible in which the name of God is not mentioned. The nearest it comes is in mentioning "another place" in Esther 4:13–14. This phrase shows that Almighty God would protect those Jews somehow! Second, Mordecai believed that Esther's beauty was not only providential—enabling her to be the queen—but that God had foreknown that all Jews would be in danger in Persia. Consequently, God put Esther in a high position for "such a time as this" (v. 14). I will add: I hope that you, reader, will have such a sense of God's guidance and providence in your life that you, too, realize that you have been preserved, kept, and prepared for such a time as this!

At this moment we see Esther's and Mordecai's finest hours. Mordecai's resistance to Haman combined with his plea and odd behavior persuaded Esther. Then, she instructed Mordecai:

> Go and assemble all the Jews who can be found in Susa and fast for me. Don't eat or drink for three days, night or day. I and my female servants will also fast in the same way. After that, I will go to the king even if it is against the law. If I perish, I perish. (v. 16)

Esther entrusted the unknown future to a known God. She risked everything she had. Here are the developments following Esther's approaching the king:

1. Queen Esther won favor in the king's sight. He asked her, "What is your request?" (5:3 ESV).
2. She asked that the king come to a banquet which had

already been prepared for him and Haman. Her request was granted (v. 5).

3. At this banquet the queen had another request, which was also granted: "If I have found favor . . . may the king and Haman come to the banquet I will prepare for them. Tomorrow I will do what the king has asked" (v. 8).
4. After Haman boasted that he had been invited again by Queen Esther to come to a feast, his wife suggested: "Have them build a gallows seventy-five feet tall. Ask the king in the morning to hang Mordecai on it" (v. 14).
5. When the king could not sleep, he asked that the book of daily events be read before him. It revealed how Mordecai had saved the king's life. The king then asked: "What honor and special recognition have been given to Mordecai for this act?" Answer: nothing (6:3).
6. Next, Haman entered the courts and the king asked him: "What should be done for the man the king wants to honor?" (6:6) Haman assumed that the king was referring to Haman himself, and so Haman gave outlandish advice that would make him look more revered and distinguished than ever. But the king replied, "Hurry" and do for Mordecai the Jew "just as you proposed. . . . Do not leave out anything you have suggested." So Haman led Mordecai through the square, proclaiming before him, "This is what is done for the man the king wants to honor" (vv. 10–11). Haman was utterly humiliated and reported everything to his wife. She gave him no comfort, foreseeing that his downfall was imminent (v. 13).

7. In the meantime, the king's eunuchs arrived and hurried to bring Haman to the feast that Esther had prepared (v. 14).
8. The king asked Esther what her request was. She revealed that the king's edict to have all Jews killed had been orchestrated by none other than Haman! Haman was now terrified before the king and queen. When the king took a walk to cool off, Haman begged the queen for mercy, then accidentally fell on her as the king walked in! This angered the king more than ever (7:1–8).
9. The king ordered Haman to be hung on the gallows that he had prepared for Mordecai. "Then the king's anger subsided" (v. 10).
10. The king gave Mordecai his signet ring which he had taken from Haman. Esther set Mordecai over the estate of Haman (8:2).
11. Esther now pleaded with the king to avert Haman's evil plan. He agreed. "The Jews celebrated with gladness, joy, and honor" (vv. 3–16).
12. All of the officials of the empire feared Mordecai and consequently helped the Jews defeat their enemies (9:3).
13. The Feast of Purim was inaugurated and has remained a Jewish feast until this day (vv. 20–32).

I doubt that "Mordecai the Jew" remotely dreamed that his awkward and strange public moaning and groaning would result in the "fear of Mordecai" one day. Nobody was afraid of Mordecai when he put on sackcloth and ashes. Nobody would predict a happy future for this pitiful man. I'm sure that Mordecai had no idea that the bitter taste of (1) being forgotten by the king,

(2) being regarded with disdain by Haman and the crowds, (3) desperately trying to get Queen Esther's attention, and then (4) asking Esther to risk her own life would give way to glory and honor. He had no idea that the king would have a sleepless night and consequently hear the document of "daily events" read to him within hours of Haman's plan to hang Mordecai. This chain of events illustrates my point about one's finest hour—you won't ever recognize it as it is happening.

The Apostle Paul would later say:

> Oh, the depth of the riches
> and the wisdom and the knowledge of God!
> How unsearchable his judgments
> and untraceable his ways!
> For who has known the mind of the Lord?
> Or who has been his counselor? (Rom. 11:33–34)

As Peter would say to those who, sadly, rejected their Messiah hundreds of years after the time of Esther:

> This Jesus is
>
> > the stone rejected by you builders,
> > which has become the cornerstone. (Acts 4:11)

Even though it does not mention the name of God, the book of Esther is especially God-centered! It is about the providence, the omniscience, and the omnipotence of God and shows how a caring God can turn things around in a very short period of time.

His purposes will ripen fast,
unfolding ev'ry hour;
The bud may have a bitter taste,
but sweet will be the flow'r.

—William Cowper

THIRTEEN

The Parents of Moses and Beating the Odds

Now a man from the family of Levi married a Levite woman. The woman became pregnant and gave birth to a son; when she saw that he was beautiful, she hid him for three months. But when she could no longer hide him, she got a papyrus basket for him and coated it with asphalt and pitch. She placed the child in it and set it among the reeds by the bank of the Nile. Then his sister stood at a distance in order to see what would happen to him.

Pharaoh's daughter went down to bathe at the Nile while her servant girls walked along the riverbank. She saw the basket among the reeds, sent her slave girl, took it, opened it, and saw him, the child—and there he was, a little boy, crying. She felt sorry for him and said, "This is one of the Hebrew boys."

Then his sister said to Pharaoh's daughter, "Should I go and call a Hebrew woman who is nursing to nurse the boy for you?"

"Go," Pharaoh's daughter told her. So the girl went and called the boy's mother. Then Pharaoh's daughter said to her, "Take this

child and nurse him for me, and I will pay your wages." So the woman took the boy and nursed him. When the child grew older, she brought him to Pharaoh's daughter, and he became her son. She named him Moses, "Because," she said, "I drew him out of the water."

—Exodus 2:1–10

By faith Moses, when he was born, was hidden for three months by his parents, because they saw that the child was beautiful, and they were not afraid of the king's edict.

—Hebrews 11:23

How little can be done under the spirit of fear.

—Florence Nightingale (1820–1910)

Bob Dylan once wrote a famous song entitled "The Times They Are a-Changin'." Indeed. Huge change can happen in a day. In an hour. Certainly in a year. What about a generational change? When the children of Israel came to live in Egypt, thanks to Joseph at the end of the book of Genesis, their future seemed secure. Joseph was loved by the pharaoh and all of Egypt. The Israelites dwelt in the fertile land of Goshen. They were loved, admired, and appreciated. Nobody looked more secure than the Israelites—as long as Joseph was alive and as long as the same pharaoh was king. But then comes one of the most sobering and ominous verses in all Holy Writ:

> A new king, who did not know about Joseph, came to power in Egypt. (Ex. 1:8)

This new king owed nothing to the previous pharaoh. He owed nothing to Joseph. And he owed nothing to the Israelites who were growing in vast numbers in Egypt. This new pharaoh said of them, "[They] are more numerous and powerful than we are." Should war ever break out, he feared they could join Egypt's enemies. The pharaoh began to oppress the Israelites, making them slaves; but they grew all the more (vv. 9–14). Their numbers increased so rapidly that a new edict ordered the killing of all male babies born to Hebrew women: "You must throw every son born to the Hebrews into the Nile, but let every daughter live" (v. 22).

Imagine how the Israelites' hearts sank. Talk about change! They could not do a single thing. Joseph was gone. No leader now cared for them. Though they were many—which was not good for them—they were lonely. They had no representation before this new king. They were utterly helpless.

Try to put yourself in the Israelites' position and imagine their ever-increasing fear. If a woman was expecting a baby, imagine the terror she felt if it turned out to be a boy. The only birth control would be total abstinence.

Times were a changin', indeed.

And then imagine the sorrow when parents had to give up their male child. Did they keep him for a few days? A week or two until the Egyptian authorities abruptly took their baby boy away?

Now we read: "A man from the family of Levi married a Levite woman" (2:1). She conceived. Endless anxiety filled the parents' hearts for the next nine months as they wondered whether their baby would be male or female.

As we will see soon, this Levite couple had deep faith in the Lord God. They were people of prayer. But I cannot imagine anything more challenging than what they went through. How would they pray for nine months—that their child would be a girl?

In this context, Moses was born. I always smile when I read these words about Moses's mother: she "saw that he was a fine child" (v. 2 ESV). Some translations say "special." Others "wonderful." Hebrews 11:23 says "beautiful." But is this not what most parents think about their new baby? The Hebrew word translated "fine" is *tov*, which means "good." Rabbi Sir David Rosen gave me his view: "I think the term means *well-behaved*. Moses's mother could see that because he was a well-behaved baby, there was a good chance that she could successfully hide him." She hid him three months. But the time came when she could hide him no longer: "she got a papyrus basket for him and coated it with asphalt and pitch" (Ex. 2:3).

I am sure that Moses's parents believed that this baby was from God and was no accident. Therefore, they trusted God to watch over him. What they did next they did "by faith"—believing God. According to my understanding of faith, this couple was given assurance that their child would be spared. "Faith is the reality of what is hoped for, the proof of what is not seen" (Heb. 11:1).

I predict confidently that when we get to heaven and get a full understanding of Old Testament events—possibly given video replays to watch (I so look forward to this)—we will find that Moses's mother and father not only prayed that God would protect their baby boy; they were New Testament examples of (1) Jesus's teaching of "believe that you have received it and it will be yours" (Mark 11:24) and (2) the Apostle John's teaching of knowing that you have prayed in the will of God. John said that if we pray in the will of God, our prayer will be answered. And if we *know* that we have prayed in the will of God, we *know* our prayer will be answered (1 John 5:14–15). That is a high level of faith. That was the faith Moses's parents had, which the writer of Hebrews refers to in Hebrews 11:23.

In a word: they believed that God would protect their child and beat the odds! After all, the odds were not great. All male babies thrown into the Nile undoubtedly drowned in seconds or suffered some other deadly fate.

When we speak about odds, we think about how probable one outcome is versus another. I am not a gambler who always tries to beat the odds in games. And my knowledge of mathematics does not extend to the nuances of probability. But common sense tells me that a lot of odds are against living a good Christian life in the 2020s. For example, we read and hear about engagements and joyful marriages only to learn a few years later that one or both parties were unfaithful, breaking that celebrated union. It is also very difficult to be fair and ethical when seeking success in business. Finally, how likely are you to release someone from a grudge you have been holding for years? Habits are deep patterns of repeated behaviors, and the odds of changing bad habits are stacked against us. Chances are that people won't get over their bad tempers. I could go on and on about how odds are not in our favor for always acting morally upright.

To put it simply: the odds are that we will not change. Jesus referred to the odds when he said:

> Enter through the narrow gate. For the gate is wide and the road broad that leads to destruction, and there are many who

> go through it. How narrow is the gate and difficult the road that leads to life, and few find it. (Matt. 7:13–14)

According to Jesus, few enter the narrow gate. And yet the Christian faith is designed to help people overcome impossible odds.

Remember that Paul said, "I am able to do all things through him who strengthens me" (Phil. 4:13).

Moses's parents had a pre-Christian taste of grace. What they perceived about baby Moses was not natural. It wasn't his physical appearance at a natural level; it was a sovereign intervention of the Holy Spirit. There is no other explanation. After all, the Holy Spirit is eternal (Heb. 9:14). The Holy Spirit was not born at Pentecost! As Bethlehem did not mark the beginning of the *Logos*, the second person of the Trinity, so Pentecost did not mark the beginning of the third person of the Trinity. The Holy Spirit, after all, was involved in creation (Gen. 1:2). Pentecost was simply the day when God chose to inaugurate the Spirit coming to the church in power. In other words, the Holy Spirit was present as much when Moses was born as he was in the days of the early church.

It is true that the Holy Spirit was "not yet given" to the disciples at one stage because Jesus was not yet glorified (John 7:39). That means that in the case of the disciples, God did not purpose to give them the same measure of the Spirit they would later receive on Pentecost after Jesus was glorified. The disciples even received another limited measure of the Spirit on Easter (20:22). That, too, does not mean that the Spirit did not exist before then or that the Spirit had never been given to people. After all, the Old Testament was written by people who were moved by the Holy Spirit (2 Peter 1:21). King David spoke specifically by the Holy Spirit when he penned Psalm 110, according to Jesus (Mark 12:36). David also pleaded with God not to take the Holy Spirit from him (Ps. 51:11). In a word: as there were preincarnate manifestations of the Son of God (e.g., Dan. 3:25), so the Holy Spirit was the explanation for *all* occasions when God did things in power!

Moses's parents were also examples of the Holy Spirit's work. This shows that the fear that the Israelites experienced was overcome by Moses's parents. They were not governed by a spirit of fear. Florence Nightingale once said that little can get done under a spirit of fear. Thankfully, "perfect love drives out fear" (1 John 4:18).

Moses's mother did a daring thing. She made a basket of bulrushes and then turned the basket into a tiny boat! She completed the boat by daubing it with bitumen and pitch. She then put the three-month-old baby in it and placed it among the reeds by the riverbank.

This was the finest hour of Moses's mother. You can be sure that she kissed the baby goodbye then hurried away, trusting God to protect him. Miriam, his sister, stood at a distance to observe what might be done to him. Lo and behold, the daughter of King Pharaoh came to the river to bathe, accompanied by her aides. She saw the basket among the reeds and sent a servant woman to open it. They saw the baby crying. She felt pity on him and said, "This is one of the Hebrew boys" (Ex. 2:6). Then followed one of the most moving, clever, and providential moments in ancient history. Miriam said to Pharaoh's daughter, "Should I go and call a Hebrew woman who is nursing to nurse the boy for you?" (v. 7).

Pharaoh's daughter said, "Go."

Miriam went and called the baby's mother who, just moments before, had kissed him goodbye! Pharaoh's daughter said to her, "Take this child and nurse him for me, and I will pay your wages." So the baby's own mother got him back and nursed him!

This is the sort of thing that only God can do. The mother gave the baby away—to God—and got him back! The baby who might have been thrown into the Nile River by the authorities now had the king's protection—the parents even getting paid! When the child grew older, his mother brought him to Pharaoh's daughter. He became her adopted son, and she named him Moses, because "I drew him out of the water" (v. 10).

Moses's parents performed an action that could have been interpreted as giving up and leaving Moses's fate to chance. But they actually believed and trusted in someone greater than King Pharaoh. This was their finest hour, when they believed in God's providence to save their son from the power of evil King Pharaoh. They didn't know how God would save, but they knew he would save.

FOURTEEN

The Parents of Jesus Putting Their Reputations on the Line

When Joseph woke up, he did as the Lord's angel had commanded him. He married her but did not have sexual relations with her until she gave birth to a son. And he named him Jesus.

—Matthew 1:24–25

His mother kept all these things in her heart.

—Luke 2:51

But he who filches from me my good name
Robs me of that which not enriches him
And makes me poor indeed.

—William Shakespeare (1564–1616)

No person on this planet is unconcerned about his or her reputation. Reputation is the general belief or opinion that other people have about you. If this concern is carried to excess, this certainly becomes sinful. It could be called having an approval addiction, that is, being consumed with perpetual worry over what people think of you. "The fear of mankind is a snare" (Prov. 29:25). Trying to please people can cause you to make faulty and foolish decisions—which you will most certainly later regret—because you are governed by the opinion you think people have of you. For instance, the Jews missed their Messiah two thousand years ago because they were preoccupied with pleasing one another rather than seeking the praise that comes from the only God (John 5:44). They didn't want to be put out of the synagogue for saying good things about Jesus (12:42). Seeking only the approval of God was not on their radar screen.

Nevertheless, there aren't many things worse than having a bad reputation. People might look down on you because you made a huge, intentional mistake or committed a shameful crime and were justly imprisoned because you raped someone, ruined another's life forever, or murdered someone and felt no sense of guilt.

And yet there is possibly something worse than any of the previous situations I just listed. That is, when people think the worst things about you *which are not true.*

The Bible describes the devil as a liar. Jesus said that when the devil lies, "he speaks from his own nature" (John 8:44). *Lying is what Satan does.* He lied to Eve in the garden of Eden. Indeed, his words are the direct opposite of the truth. God said to Adam and Eve that if they partook of the forbidden fruit, they would die (Gen. 2:17). Eve quoted that word to Satan, who countered immediately: "You will certainly not die" (3:4). This is why Jesus gave him the name "father of lies" (John 8:44). Whereas God is truth (Ps. 33:4) and it is impossible for God to lie (Heb. 6:18), Satan lies for a living.

These things said, when the "time came to completion" (Gal. 4:4), that is, moments just before the eternal *Logos* entered the womb of the Virgin Mary, God's plan was unfolding. And the challenges to the reputations of Mary and Joseph were a part of that plan.

The teenaged virgin Mary was suddenly visited by an angel in Nazareth of Galilee. It was the angel Gabriel—"sent by God"—presumably the same angel who spoke to Daniel (Dan. 8:15–26; 9:20–23). Gabriel went to a young girl who was engaged and said, "Greetings." Oh my! Never in the history of the world had such a greeting been given! It seems such an understated, lack-luster word. But since some word presumably had to be used, I suppose "Greetings" would be as good as any.

> Greetings, favored woman! The Lord is with you. (Luke 1:28)

Mary was both troubled and afraid—who wouldn't be? She tried to discern what kind of greeting this might be. The angel said,

> Do not be afraid, Mary, for you have found favor with God. Now listen: You will conceive and give birth to a son, and you will name him Jesus. He will be great and will be called the Son of the Most High, and the Lord God will give

> him the throne of his father David. He will reign over the house of Jacob forever, and his kingdom will have no end. (vv. 30–33)

I cannot help but wonder whether Mary had an intimate relationship with God—and was consequently favored—or if God sovereignly chose Mary. In the latter case, God's favor of Mary had nothing to do with her godliness.

Whatever the case may be, this was a lot of information for Mary to take in. The Gospel of Luke portrays this interchange quickly—it may have occurred in only a few seconds. But this overwhelming news would take most of us more than a few seconds to absorb. Either this teenaged girl was a quick thinker or perhaps Luke is summarizing the account to a few seconds. Or, maybe, Mary did indeed have a moment or two—maybe a few minutes—to absorb this news. We are not talking merely about an event that would change a young lady's life forever, but a momentous change in world history! The life Mary would carry in her womb would eventually change how we measure time—between BC and AD. Indeed, this was the greatest and most historic moment in the history and development of the entire world!

Apparently, Mary realized the implications. She knew that she and Joseph had not slept together. "What exactly is going on?" Mary said to the angel:

> How can this be, since I have not had sexual relations with a man? (v. 34)

Fair question. So the angel answered her:

> The Holy Spirit will come upon you, and the power of the Most High will overshadow you. Therefore, the holy one to be born will be called the Son of God. (v. 35)

Assuming Luke is not summarizing but repeating verbatim what Gabriel continued to say to her, Mary now learns about her cousin Elizabeth (v. 36). Gabriel had gone some six months before to Zechariah to let him know his prayer had been answered. He had likely been praying for a son for about twenty-five years (v. 13). Zechariah wanted to argue with Gabriel (a rather stupid thing to do), implying there had to be a big mistake since both he and his wife Elizabeth were old. Zechariah was consequently struck dumb—not able to speak. But his unbelief did not abort the answer to his prayer (v. 20).

Mary's cousin Elizabeth was now six months pregnant. The angel added, "For nothing will be impossible with God" (v. 37). My question is, did Gabriel share these words with Mary to increase her faith? Did this news of Elizabeth being pregnant in her old age help Mary to take in what Gabriel was telling her?

I don't think Mary was anxiously wondering in that moment if people in her hometown of Nazareth would accuse her of being pregnant before she and Joseph were married. But we do know that Mary's faith was strong and that she was ready to listen to Gabriel and go along with the next thing to happen. "See, I am the Lord's servant . . . may it happen to me as you have said" (v. 38). Quicker than one can bat an eyelash, the baby Jesus was in Mary's womb.

We don't know if Gabriel gave further instructions to Mary. For example, was she instructed to keep this virgin birth a secret—the best-kept secret ever? Or did Mary have by nature such tremendous wisdom that she would not share what had happened—except to her fiancé Joseph? Luke tells us that Mary "kept all these things in her heart" (2:51). These words seem to imply that the event described by both Luke and Matthew had been kept a secret.

SILENT HEROES

Mary had a difficult task on her hands. She had to share this extraordinary news of her virgin pregnancy with Joseph. The worst scenario imaginable must have entered Joseph's mind. He might have initially thought that she had been unfaithful to him. Matthew implies that Joseph did not take the news well at first: being a "righteous man," that is, he did not want to disgrace her publicly (Matt. 1:19), Joseph planned to call off the engagement quietly. But a gracious God, who is never too late and never too early, but always is just on time, sent an angel to Joseph. Was this angel also Gabriel? Probably. We only know that an angel of the Lord appeared to Joseph in a dream, saying:

> Joseph, son of David, don't be afraid to take Mary as your wife, because what has been conceived in her is from the Holy Spirit. She will give birth to a son, and you are to name him Jesus, because he will save his people from their sins. (vv. 20–21)

When Joseph woke up, he did as the angel of the Lord had commanded him. Not only did he please Mary, but he welcomed the stigma that he would bear the rest of his life. He took her as his wife, but did not sleep with her until she had given birth to a son. However, Joseph was also given the dignity of naming the baby: "And he named him Jesus" (v. 25).

We don't know if Joseph was warned that he should not reveal these details to anyone. "A good name is to be chosen over great wealth" (Prov. 22:1). But the moment Joseph agreed to stay with Mary, he forfeited having a good name, and perhaps a good reputation, for the rest of his life. He was not allowed to tell the truth. Or was it a case of realizing that no one would believe him, so why tell it?

A pregnant woman can only hide the outward signs of pregnancy for so long. People eventually ask questions—"Are you pregnant?" "When is the baby due?" In this case, it would not be surprising if people wondered how Mary had become pregnant and if Joseph was the father. Mary and Joseph, however, kept quiet. They chose to deal with the stigma. The circumstances of Jesus's birth were not an issue for his disciples in any way. But, as we will see, they were significant for his enemies. And yet, as far as I am aware, the truth about Mary's virginity was not widely known until Luke and Matthew revealed it in Holy Writ—a generation later!

"Silence is true wisdom's best reply," noted Euripides (480–406 BC). But keeping utterly quiet sometimes takes enormous courage. Joseph and Mary were bound to stay silent. In doing so, they became consummate examples of people who would refuse to defend themselves or clear their names. *Their silence was their finest hour.*

"Vengeance and retribution belong to me" (Deut. 32:35). Vindication was and is and always will be God's prerogative. Refusing to vindicate oneself, to clear one's name, or to make oneself look good is the quintessence of godliness. God himself is the most hated, the most unvindicated, the most misunderstood, and the most accused person in the universe. Yet he absolutely refuses to clear his name. Indeed, this is the ultimate test of a loyal follower of the God of the Bible. You and I must be willing to never—ever—clear our names.

I would say to you, dear reader, that it is only a matter of time before you, too, will be put to this test. What if people lie about you? What if the devil, the father of liars, manages to turn people against you? What if he spreads lies about you to make you look horrible? He is preoccupied with the nonstop task of making God look bad. He will get you to question the inspiration of the Bible. He will get you to doubt the literal resurrection of Jesus from the dead. He will get you to deny the gospel—either by embellishing it in making you think you must produce good works to be saved or by getting you to reject it entirely. He will get you to doubt the existence of hell. Finally, he will get you to believe not in the God of the Bible, but a "God" people are comfortable with—a God who does not punish sin, a God who is likeable, a God who does not require holiness, and a God who is nothing like the God of the Bible.

However, the God of the Bible is all-powerful and knows everything. The God of the Bible is a jealous God. The God of the Bible sent his one and only Son to die on a cross and shed his blood to satisfy the wrath and justice of God. After all, the angel said to Joseph that Jesus would save his people from their sins (Matt. 1:21). The message of the cross was, therefore, immediately introduced to the adopted father of Jesus. The God of the Bible sent his Holy Spirit to enable you and me to have a close and real relationship with him. We do this by simultaneously fearing him and loving him.

The Lord "confides" in those who fear him, said David (Ps. 25:14 NIV). The King James Version says, "The secret of the LORD is with them that fear him." Not many people can keep a secret, and I sometimes think the Lord would show us more of himself if we could keep quiet about it. There is a time to be unashamed of the Lord—and witness for him. But there is also a time to keep quiet about the Lord confiding in us. Nevertheless, most of us want to blab out such secrets—not to make the Lord look good, but to make ourselves look good.

Joseph and Mary were brilliant, if I may put it that way, because they were willing to keep quiet about what they knew to be true.

Joseph and Mary abandoned vindication by keeping silent. They would forfeit having a good name from the beginning. They were not allowed to tell the truth—they made this decision either by instructions from God or on their own. Joseph would be known as the man who got a teenage girl pregnant. This was thrown up years later when would-be followers of Jesus began to dislike him. After Jesus refused to let the people make him king (John 6:15), they began to find fault with his teaching (v. 41). Suddenly, the rumors of some thirty years which had been overlooked were now taken with both hands! The people said, "Isn't this Jesus the son of Joseph, whose father and mother we know?" (v. 42).

Even Jesus himself bore the stigma of being an illegitimate child. I am sure he knew that he was born of Mary when she was a virgin. Did Mary tell him? Probably. Did God his Father tell him? Probably. A huge christological question concerns when Jesus first became self-conscious of his deity.

Joseph bore the stigma of being a man who could not

discipline himself to abstain from sleeping with Mary until they were married. Mary equally bore the stigma of being an unwed mother. Their glory was in the untelling of what they knew.

When it comes to God's timing in vindication, always remember two principles: (1) only the *truth* will be vindicated; and (2) true vindication is only guaranteed in the life to come. As Paul put it in 1 Corinthians 4:5: "So don't judge anything prematurely, before the Lord comes, who will both bring to light what is hidden in darkness and reveal the intentions of the hearts. And then praise will come to each one from God."

The essential principle of vindication is this: you and I must be willing to abandon any vindication *in this life*. We get our joy from knowing the truth. Joseph and Mary could live with themselves, for they knew the truth.

FIFTEEN

David, a Man after God's Heart

Then the king instructed Zadok, "Return the ark of God to the city. If I find favor with the Lord, *he will bring me back and allow me to see both it and its dwelling place. However, if he should say, 'I do not delight in you,' then here I am—he can do with me whatever pleases him."*

—2 Samuel 15:25–26

Genuine people are rare. If you can't find one, be one.

—Anonymous

I preached through the life of David when I was pastor at Westminster Chapel. From September to December, I covered the "glory days" of David as king—from the beginning of his kingship to the time of his sins of adultery and murder and subsequent exposure by Nathan the prophet in 2 Samuel 12.

However, during the Christmas break I made a decision not to continue with the life of David.

"Why?" asked the deacons.

"I don't have the stomach for it," I replied. "The 'downside' of David is so depressing. I just can't go through with it."

On the first Wednesday of the new year Westminster Chapel had a day of prayer and fasting. To be honest, I wasn't expecting much of anything. Until this point in my spiritual life, fasting had left me thinking "don't expect anything." But this time things felt different.

As I fasted, to my surprise I suddenly heard these words: "So you aren't going to complete your preaching on the life of David? Do you not realize that that is where your people are?"

I was shocked. This was a wake-up call for me. So I resumed the David series the following Sunday, the title of my message being, "The Downside of the Life of David," kicking off the second part of David's life from 2 Samuel 13 to 24. I can tell you, I actually enjoyed preaching on the latter half of David's life more than his "glory days."

Here is what I learned: I discovered what type of man David was. It has troubled me for so long to think that David was called "a man after God's own heart" in both the Old and New Testaments (1 Sam. 13:14, Acts 13:22). Here's a man whose sin of adultery and murder is arguably worse than any other sinful act in the entire Bible! How could someone who sinned like that be called a man after God's own heart?

Two incidents from David's life gave me perspective.

First, David *accepted and endured* the chastening of the Lord for his sin. The testing in the fire reveals the true character of a person, and God inflicted unthinkably great chastening upon David. Nathan uncovered David's sin and then prophesied:

> "You struck down Uriah the Hethite with the sword and took his wife as your own wife—you murdered him with the Ammonite's sword. Now therefore, the sword will never leave your house because you despised me and took the wife of Uriah the Hethite to be your own wife."
>
> This is what the LORD says, "I am going to bring disaster on you from your own family: I will take your wives and give them to another before your very eyes, and he will sleep with them in broad daylight. You acted in secret, but I will do this before all Israel and in broad daylight." (2 Sam. 12:9–12)

Was David angry with Nathan?

Was he rebellious?

Was he defensive?

The answer to all three questions was, "No."

David obviously felt horrible and was utterly repentant. His immediate response was: "I have sinned against the LORD" (v. 13).

Here is David's prayer after being found out by Nathan:

> Be gracious to me, God,
> according to your faithful love;
> according to your abundant compassion,
> blot out my rebellion.
> Completely wash away my guilt
> and cleanse me from my sin.
> For I am conscious of my rebellion,

and my sin is always before me.
Against you—you alone—I have sinned
and done this evil in your sight.
So you are right when you pass sentence;
you are blameless when you judge. (Ps. 51:1–4)

We can't say for sure how soon David prayed this prayer after his abasement. We know what transpired after Nathan's prediction that bad things would happen to David:

1. David's son Amnon raped his own sister Tamar.
2. Absalom, another son of David, killed his brother Amnon in revenge.
3. Absalom fled to Geshur, but later returned to Jerusalem.
4. Absalom stole the hearts of the people and made himself king.
5. David fled from Jerusalem and went into exile, knowing that Nathan's prophetic word continued to be fulfilled.

Why is telling this story important? It shows that God gives second chances. It shows that those who have messed up and think that they can no longer come into God's inheritance for them may indeed come into their inheritance and have a reward in heaven. Let no one reading this chapter imagine that he or she must give up hope for a brilliant future due to having committed sins—including serious sins.

If David can be a man after God's own heart, so can you. Whom the Lord loves, he chastens—or disciplines (Heb. 12:6). If you have displeased God and experienced severe consequences, be encouraged. If God used David after his horrible sin, he can use you. If you can be like David was when he endured his worst pain, you have every reason to hope that God is not finished with you either.

Second, David made a decision to honor God above his own kingship. It is my opinion that what follows describes the greatest and most transparent demonstration of pure godliness to be found in the Old Testament. One might say that David's committal of the worst sin of the Old Testament was matched by David's greatest act of humility.

The priests Zadok and Abiathar wanted to show the greatest possible sign of loyalty to David, their king and friend, since they knew that Absalom's stealing of the kingship was wrong. All the people respected them. More than that, these priests knew the reverence and glory associated with the ark of the covenant, which symbolized God's presence. Since only these priests had access to the ark, they had a good plan that would get the people in Jerusalem to stick by David if the ark was with him. They believed that the ark alongside David would mean that God was on David's side. In a word: Zadok and Abiathar believed they could win the kingship back for David by using the ark.

This was David's darkest and bleakest hour. His sorrow, his personal hurt, his depression, and his tears were part of his punishment. And yet his depth of repentance toward God outweighed every other emotion he had. He had let God down, and he felt this keenly. He had failed God—big time—and this hurt him the most. He knew that everything happening to him was by God's own instigation. He was set against arguing with God or trying to manipulate the situation for his benefit.

Zadok and Abiathar, however, wanted to send a decisive signal to all Israelites and Jerusalemites that God was still with

David. Not only Zadok and Abiathar, but "all the Levites" supported this plan (2 Sam. 15:24).

Zadok and Abiathar chose priests who would legally carry the ark in a way that no one physically touched it—through poles on their shoulders. Abiathar and Zadok now followed David and some six hundred of his loyal followers across the Kidron. When the ark was set down, the priest Abiathar offered sacrifices.

Recall the construction of the ark. Moses did not guess how to make it; he followed the literal instructions from the Most High God, building a "copy" (Heb. 8:5) of the ark as a shadow of the heavenly reality (Ex. 25:10–22). On the top of the ark—a wooden chest approximately four by three feet long—was a slab of gold called the "mercy seat." Only the high priest could enter the holy of holies where the ark would reside inside the Tent of Meeting. God had a high purpose for the ark: "I will meet with you there" (v. 22).

The ark had once been captured by the Philistines—and God struck their god Dagon face down before it (1 Sam. 5:4). The terrified Philistines then returned the ark to Israel. However, right away at least seventy Israelites were struck dead by looking into it (6:19). Moreover, when King David later had the ark moved to Jerusalem, Uzzah reached out to it because the oxen carrying it stumbled. He was struck dead on the spot (2 Sam. 6:7). David and his people then realized they had not shown proper reverence to God and consequently made sure that no further person touched the ark. When the ark was finally safely brought to Jerusalem, this occasion was one of David's most thrilling moments (vv. 17–19).

It would be impossible to exaggerate the hallowed history of the ark. That is why taking the ark out of Jerusalem merely to follow David was a most extraordinary occurrence.

However, David's worst moment became his finest hour. After Abiathar offered sacrifices, David gave this surprising command to Zadok:

> "Return the ark of God to the city. If I find favor with the Lord, he will bring me back and allow me to see both it and its dwelling place. However, if he should say, 'I do not delight in you,' then here I am—he can do with me whatever pleases him."
>
> . . . So Zadok and Abiathar returned the ark of God to Jerusalem and stayed there." (15:25–26, 29)

David showed that he was not superstitious about the presence of the ark. David did not want the ark next to him; he wanted God's own approval. There were those present who might have thought that one could control God by controlling the Ark. Not David—he wanted God.

David's remarkable decision to send the ark back to the city plus his words that the Lord can "do what seems good to him" demonstrate deep love and honor and *trust* in the sovereign will of God—no greater instance of this can be imagined. That is why this was David's finest hour. He risked everything without any guarantee of reward or esteem, thinking only of God's glory and honor.

SIXTEEN

Rebekah and Applying God's Word

And the Lord *said to [Rebekah]:*

Two nations are in your womb;
two peoples will come from you and be separated.
One people will be stronger than the other,
and the older will serve the younger.
—Genesis 25:23

True wisdom is found in trusting God
when you can't figure things out.
—Joni Eareckson Tada

It is very special when you hear God speak. That is, you know in your heart of hearts that you just heard from God by the Holy Spirit. Rebekah, Isaac's wife, knew that God had spoken to her when, after being barren for years, she became pregnant with twins.

It is not clear to me whether Rebekah told Isaac what God told her in Genesis 25, namely, that the elder of the twins would serve the younger. Surely she would, I would have thought. The word from the Holy Spirit indicated that God had chosen Jacob over Esau. In any case, after the birth of the twins Isaac preferred Esau over Jacob, but Rebekah loved Jacob more than Esau. Like it or not, this is what Holy Scripture states. I have taught that a parent showing favoritism is not a good thing. But favoritism was practiced by the patriarchs, and we must accept that this happened. In the case of Jacob and Esau, Joni Eareckson Tada says, "True wisdom is found in trusting God when you can't figure things out." The reason for Isaac's preference for Esau is not stated in Scripture; perhaps it was because Esau was the firstborn.

I sympathize with Rebekah. It is doubtful that her preference for Jacob would have arisen apart from the word from God to her. I therefore take the view that Rebekah's persuasion of Jacob to deceive Isaac was motivated by what had been revealed to her supernaturally. Moreover, she believed that she was responsible to bring about the prediction that God gave her. Rebekah did not ask for such a revelation, but felt that God had told her for a reason. As we will see soon, the beginning of the doctrine of predestination is shown in this incident. In other words, Rebekah did not take the view that "what is to be will be, whether it happens or not"! She believed that God had given this revelation to her for a purpose and that it was her responsibility to apply it. She saw that *applying* God's word was her duty since it was God's idea that (1) she was given this information before the birth of the twins and (2) Jacob was chosen by God rather than Esau. Who could blame Rebekah for making this deduction?

Twice in Holy Writ we have the words, "I loved Jacob, but I hated Esau" (Mal. 1:2–3, Rom. 9:13). Why did this happen? Why would God choose Jacob rather than Esau before they were born? You tell me. Was it necessary for Rebekah to step in and help determine the future of Jacob? She thought so. There is not a word in Holy Scripture criticizing her involvement.

It would seem that God who predestines the end also predestines the means to the end. This being true, Rebekah saw herself as God's chosen means to ensure that the patriarchal blessing be directed to the younger son—Jacob.

Paul unfolds the doctrine of predestination in Romans 8 and 9, using the story of Jacob and Esau. He could not have been clearer:

> For though [Jacob and Esau] had not been born yet or done anything good or bad, so that God's purpose according to election might stand—not from works but from the one who calls—[Rebekah] was told, **The older will serve the younger.** As it is written: **I have loved Jacob, but I have hated Esau.** (Rom. 9:11–13)

Years ago, I asked my Greek professor at seminary (who was vigorously anti-predestination in his theology), "If Paul wanted to say that God chose the elect by his own will and not because he foresaw their faith, but did not make this clear, how might he have said it to be clearer?"

The professor replied, "Oh, Paul said it clearly enough. I just disagree with Paul."

I don't know of anyone who naturally likes the teaching of predestination. The possible exception would be those who were brought up to believe it. That way, they normally say nothing very critical about it. We all tend to accept things as we grow up—whether in Siberia, India, or Kentucky. Those outside these areas tend to ask those who are from these areas, "How did you stand it?" The same would be true in how we think theologically. We tend to ask, "How could you believe such a thing?"

Scripture doesn't tell us very much about Rebekah. When Abraham's servant came to her home to find a wife for Isaac, she agreed to go with him at once (Gen. 24:58). She was barren for a long time. We know that she prayed to the Lord on her own. She seemed to be against her husband Isaac's preference. This makes me think that she never told Isaac about God's word to her before the twins were born. In any case, she had a mind of her own!

But when God opened Rebekah's womb, she became pregnant with twins. Rebekah felt them jostling inside her and was worried, so she asked God why this was happening. God replied:

> Two nations are in your womb;
> two peoples will come from you and be separated.
> One people will be stronger than the other,
> and the older will serve the younger. (25:23)

Why would the Lord tell her this? Why not tell it to Isaac? You tell me. This news was not Rebekah's idea—it was entirely God's idea. This means that predestination is God's idea. No human being—certainly a fallen creature—would have come up with such a thought. I suspect that the only way a person can like predestination is when he or she believes that it is God's idea. If we love God, we love what he does and how he thinks.

Therefore, the one big thing in Rebekah's life that many would not applaud would be the way she manipulated Jacob to deceive his father. When she overheard Isaac tell Esau to prepare his favorite food for him so that he could give Esau his patriarchal blessing, Rebekah then ordered Jacob:

> Obey my voice as I command you. Go to the flock and bring me two good young goats, so that I may prepare from them delicious food for your father, such as he loves. And you shall bring it to your father to eat, so that he may bless you before he dies. (27:8–10 ESV)

Note that Rebekah *commands* Jacob. Why should Rebekah care? Why would this situation be so important? This is a daring thing to do. But her instructions to Jacob would never have been given had not the Lord himself given her a private revelation in advance that Jacob would be the favored son. Rebekah gave her command in obedience to the Lord.

Rebekah was so earnest for the blessing to go to Jacob and thus fulfill the word of the Lord to her that she would deceive her husband. Don't get me wrong—I am not saying that spouses should look for ways to deceive one another. But this risk tells me that Rebekah was a person that believed she had to bring about the word of the Lord.

Jacob, however, caught between his mother and father, was reluctant to carry out Rebekah's order because he feared that his father would find out: "My brother Esau is a hairy man, but I am a man with smooth skin. Suppose my father touches me. Then I will be revealed to him as a deceiver and bring a curse rather than a blessing on myself" (vv. 11–12).

Then came Rebekah's boldest and most courageous word yet: "Your curse be on me, my son. Just obey me and go get [the goats] for me" (v. 13).

This was Rebekah's finest hour. She believed the word of the Lord so deeply that she swore an oath to her son: "Your curse be on me."

The scenario unfolds like a drama, including some nail-biting tension. Will Rebekah's plan of deception work?

Rebekah put skins of young goats on Jacob's hands and on the smooth part of his neck. She put the delicious food into the hands of her son Jacob. Then she nudged Jacob in the direction of his blind father and Jacob said, "I am Esau, your firstborn. I have done as you told me. Please sit up and eat some of my game so that you may bless me."

Jacob must have been very nervous when Isaac said to him, "How did you ever find it [the game which Isaac asked Esau for] so quickly, my son?"

Jacob replied with another lie: "Because the Lord your God made it happen for me."

Feeling unsure, Isaac said to Jacob, "Please come closer so I can touch you, my son. Are you really my son Esau or not?" Oh, dear. Jacob complies and hears Isaac say, "The voice is the voice of Jacob, but the hands are the hands of Esau." Begging for reassurance, Isaac asked, "Are you really my son Esau?"

Jacob lied again: "I am."

Then Isaac blessed Jacob. He ate the game which Rebekah

had prepared. "Please come closer and kiss me, my son." Jacob did (vv. 14–27).

Earlier in this book when we looked at Isaac's finest hour, remember when Esau finally showed up to get the patriarchal blessing? Isaac did not take back the blessing he had given to Jacob. That was another hard truth to accept.

Regarding the doctrine of predestination, whereas Romans 9:11 places the responsibility on God; Hebrews 12:16 puts it on Esau. In between was Rebekah applying the word that God gave her.

How should we deal with this? Should we see this as what God decreed or what Esau foolishly did? Answer: both. This is where the term "antinomy" comes into play. The late theologian Dr. J. I. Packer takes this word from the eighteenth-century philosopher Immanuel Kant to help unravel the mystery of God's sovereignty and man's responsibility. Of course, this mystery can never be totally explained in this life. I wouldn't even try, if I were you. That said, an antinomy is this (as I understand it): two parallel principles that are irreconcilable but both true.

If you are sound in your Christology, you actually already accept the idea of antinomy. For example, you believe that Jesus was and is God. Simultaneously, you believe that Jesus was and is a human being. Does that mean he was fifty percent God and fifty percent man? No! He was one hundred percent God and one hundred percent human. Figure this out. You can't. I suppose the antinomy idea is an attempt to "figure out" things. But I bring this concept in to show that if you can accept the antinomy when it comes to the person of Jesus, perhaps you can accept it regarding the mystery of God's sovereignty.

Moses wanted to figure out how a bush could be on fire and

not burn up. As he came closer to the burning bush, God said, "STOP. Take off your shoes. You are on holy ground" (Ex. 3:5, my paraphrase). God does not want us to try to figure out what he does not want us to figure out.

My view, then, is that we should respect God and not try to untangle these puzzles. For her part, Rebekah didn't try to figure things out. She was convinced that God had chosen Jacob over Esau because God had revealed this to her. Her finest hour was applying what God told her even if that meant she would be cursed. She applied the teaching of predestination as though it were up to her. That is what many who hold strong views on both evangelism and the sovereignty of God believe. The eighteenth-century evangelist George Whitefield is a good example of this. We should dignify belief in the sovereignty of God by trying to save the lost as if it were up to us.

Rebekah did make strange and foolish decisions. I would never advise partners to keep information from one another secret. I also wouldn't advocate lying. But Rebekah is also a good example of someone who is willing to risk being cursed in order to believe what the Lord says. We need to honor such a firm faith in God's promises.

SEVENTEEN

Elisha and Abandoning Vindication

Then Naaman and his whole company went back to the man of God, stood before him, and declared, "I know there's no God in the whole world except in Israel. Therefore, please accept a gift from your servant."

But Elisha said, "As the LORD lives, in whose presence I stand, I will not accept it." Naaman urged him to accept it, but he refused.

—2 Kings 5:15–16

I'm only responsible for what I say or do, not for what you hear or understand.

—Anonymous

When a feller says, 'It ain't the money, it's the principle, it's the money'," as we would say back in the hills of Kentucky. "When it comes to money, everybody's religion is the same," said Voltaire (1694–1778). "The last part of a person to be converted is his wallet," added John Wesley (1703–1791). According to the second-century document known as the *Didache*, "the teaching of the twelve disciples," one way to discern between a false prophet or a true one was: "If he asks for money, he is a false prophet." The Apostle Paul also warned: "The love of money is a root of all kinds of evil" (1 Tim. 6:10). And, finally, the Apostle Peter cautioned that pastors should beware of leading the flock "out of greed for money" (1 Peter 5:2).

My focus in this chapter is the prophet Elisha and his servant Gehazi. Elisha was not controlled by money, but Gehazi was.

This chapter is not really about money—but money is connected to the main topic. The larger issue is about how people seek to protect their reputations. Money, sex, and power are among the things that the child of God must get the victory over. Or, as some would put it: the gold, the girls, and the glory.

Elisha was the successor to Elijah. He had asked Elijah for a double portion of his spirit—and got it (2 Kings 2:6–14). What is meant by "double portion" is somewhat mysterious. There were approximately seven miraculous accounts in the ministry of Elijah and around fourteen in that of Elisha, depending on how you evaluate each of them. "Beauty is to the eye of the beholder"—so what I regard as the greatest or most remarkable miracle in Elisha's ministry may differ from your choice. But my vote for Elisha's greatest miracle is the healing of Naaman the leper, the Syrian general.

Naaman and Elisha's relationship got off to a rocky start. Naaman first went to see Elisha for healing and expected to meet the prophet face to face. After all, Naaman was the commander for the king of Aram. But Elisha did not greet Naaman, instead sending a strange secondhand word to him containing unusual instructions to dip in the Jordan River seven times. Naaman felt insulted; his position as commander made him accustomed to special treatment. Naaman was angry for two reasons: (1) he thought that the prophet would feel honored to at least greet him, and (2) the instructions seemed utterly ridiculous to him.

After his servants managed to convince him, Naaman finally climbed down and humbly dipped himself seven times in the Jordan per Elisha's instructions. When he came up the seventh time, "his skin was restored and became like the skin of a small boy, and he was clean" (5:14). Naaman was filled with gratitude and returned to Elisha's home to show his thanks. This time, Naaman met the prophet and affirmed the God of Israel by saying, "I know there's no God in the whole world except in Israel. Therefore, please accept a gift from your servant" (v. 15).

Surprisingly, Elisha refused this gift. Elisha was not motivated by the love of money; he would not take anything at all. We do not know why Elisha rejected a financial gift, but he probably wanted to ensure that no one outside of Israel could say that the prophets of Israel could be bought. Elisha wanted Naaman to know that God's goodness cannot be bought with money.

Unfortunately Gehazi, Elisha's servant, had other thoughts. Gehazi knew that Naaman had come to Israel with a lot of money, which he was prepared to spend to get healed. Gehazi should have known better, but, sadly, he caught up with Naaman's chariot before the general had gone far from Elisha's house and lied to him. The greedy Gehazi said to Naaman that Elisha had changed his mind and would now take a gift. Of course, Naaman then gave Gehazi what he asked for, then headed on his way back home, believing he had been able to reward Elisha for his miraculous healing after all. This was a stupid thing for Gehazi to do; did he think that the great prophet would not have discerned this bad act? God consequently struck Gehazi with Naaman's leprosy (vv. 20–27).

One time Gehazi happened to visit the king of Israel. The king said to Gehazi, "Tell me all the great things Elisha has done" (8:4). Every time I read this passage in 2 Kings I am reminded about how I used to retell stories of the miraculous ministries of Arthur Blessitt and Paul Cain. These stories are amazing. We have no way of knowing exactly what stories Gehazi related. I can imagine, however, that he would tell the king some of these:

- how bad water was made sweet (2:21–22)
- how a widow's oil was multiplied (4:1–7)
- how a barren woman was given a son within a year (4:11–17)
- how the same son was raised from the dead (4:18–37)
- how deadly stew was made good (4:38–41)
- how bread was multiplied (4:42–44)
- how Naaman the leper was healed (5:1–14)

When I preached on the life of Elisha, I was moved most of all by what is *missing* in the Naaman story. Elisha did not make Gehazi go back to Naaman to explain that Elisha had not instructed Gehazi to ask for money. This amazes me; I would have commanded Gehazi to go back.

Elisha allowed Naaman to believe that he gave Elisha money—the opposite to the way Elisha conducted himself.

The greater point is not that Elisha refused money but that he let Naaman believe he accepted money. Elisha neither wanted nor needed Naaman's money. And he let Naaman think that he did want the money by not commanding Gehazi to tell Naaman the truth. Did Elisha want to spare Naaman embarrassment? Maybe.

Nevertheless, this was Elisha's finest hour.

It has been said, "I am only responsible by what I say or do, not for what you hear or understand." Elisha was not responsible for what Naaman now assumed to be true. This is important because it shows that Elisha was getting joy from *knowing that only God knows*! It coalesces neatly with John 5:44: "How can you believe, since you accept glory from one another but don't seek the glory that comes from the only God?"

The reason that the Elisha–Naaman episode gripped me is because it is so far removed from what I would have done. I am ashamed to admit that I fear that I would have made an effort to clear my name! I would not cope well with Naaman's final takeaway of the situation. Naaman would have said to himself, "Fair enough that Elisha would take a gift." He probably didn't think less of Elisha for taking his money. But he would never again hold Elisha in high esteem for refusing the gift.

For his part, Elisha would have almost certainly gotten some satisfaction from refusing Naaman's gift. But, in the end, Gehazi blew it. However, Elisha did not command Gehazi to retract what had happened, because Elisha was more upset about Gehazi's love for money and for his compromising the testimony about God's free goodness that Elisha wanted to leave with Naaman. If Elisha was indeed upset that Naaman now thought Elisha accepted money, who knows? I would have been upset myself, after all. None of us would enjoy someone believing something about us that is not a compliment.

Elisha's allowing Naaman to think what is not true—in this case—is true godliness and true humility. It is an example of being truly self-effacing—truly losing your life for the glory of God. If what I suspected about Elisha was true, that he didn't want the surrounding nations to think that Israel's prophets could be bought, then it was a big deal and exercise in humility for Elisha to allow Naaman to think that he had paid him. Elisha did not try to clear his name; only God knew that Elisha didn't try to take the money. This is what Jesus called taking the "lowest" seat (Luke 14:10).

Elisha, by nature, was an ambitious man. Only an ambitious man would ask for a double portion of Elijah's anointing! Martin Luther is quoted as saying that God uses sex to drive a man to marriage, ambition to drive a man to service, and fear to drive a man to faith. As the *eros* love that makes a man want to get married must be paralleled—not replaced—by *agape* love for the marriage to be happy, so our ambition must be channeled in such a way that we love God's glory more than earthly praise. Elisha was also a proud man. When some kids made fun of his bald head, he sent a curse on them (2 Kings 2:23–24). It is reasonable to assume that Elisha had thoughts about what Naaman now believed about him. But in the end, he refused to do anything about it.

For those of us who are proud and ambitious, including myself, we learn here that the satisfaction of pleasing God is much greater than the satisfaction of another's admiration or approval.

Would you like to get on a fast track to please God? Get your satisfaction from knowing that God knows. Get your comfort from this. Get your ego strength from this. Get your joy from this. *God knows.* God knows what we know; he also knows what we don't know.

What Naaman thought doesn't matter. Elisha never had a strategy to please the Syrian general in the first place! He lived to please the Lord. He got his joy from pleasing God. Reader, I would urge you to seek satisfaction not from God pleasing you but you pleasing him. And when you feel robbed of the satisfaction of knowing that people respect you, remember this: God knows, and he knows the truth.

When we have been maligned, hurt, persecuted, or falsely accused, we must learn to get our satisfaction not from telling people what hurtful or unfair treatment was inflicted upon us by others, but by taking a page from the old spiritual:

> Nobody knows the troubles I've seen;
> Nobody knows but Jesus.

Elisha lived to please and honor God. He took his instructions from God. He received his anointing from God. He was indebted to God. If Elisha was bothered for a moment that Naaman now believed that he had given money to him, he would have dismissed his own concerns in a second by realizing that *God knows.* God knows how we feel and care. *That* is what really matters.

EIGHTEEN

Paul and Standing Alone

Then Paul replied, "What are you doing, weeping and breaking my heart? For I am ready not only to be bound but also to die in Jerusalem for the name of the Lord Jesus."

Since he would not be persuaded, we said no more except, "The Lord's will be done."

—Acts 21:13–14

At the final judgment, everyone will stand before God alone.

—R. C. Sproul (1939–2017)

I want to remind the reader of my definition of "finest hour." It is a person's most self-effacing moment. It is when you are not trying to impress anybody. It is when you are even willing to look bad in another's eyes; indeed, you only care about God's opinion. I remind you of this because when it comes to the Apostle Paul's finest hour, it would be easy to rush to examples in his life that might qualify. Some might say it is Saul's conversion on the road to Damascus. That was certainly a *defining* moment, but any self-effacing indication—e.g., when Saul said, "What should I do, Lord?" (Acts 22:10)—would actually be the result of irresistible grace! In contrast, I think one's finest hour is a voluntary decision. A case could be made that Paul's finest hour was in his last letter and word to Timothy: "I have fought the good fight, I have finished the race, I have kept the faith" (2 Tim. 4:7). These words reveal Paul's honesty but not necessarily his humility. The same situation possibly applies also to Paul's words "I have been crucified with Christ" (Gal. 2:20) or when he puts down his pedigree and wishes only to know Christ and the power of his resurrection and the fellowship of his sufferings (Phil. 3:7–10). There are no doubt other episodes. Which particular episode in Paul's life is his finest hour?

The book of Acts tells us that Paul was utterly determined to go to Jerusalem. But nobody agreed that he should go. He addressed the elders of the church in Ephesus, noting that this would be the last time he would see them:

> I am on my way to Jerusalem, compelled by the Spirit, not knowing what I will encounter there, except that in every town the Holy Spirit warns me that chains and afflictions are waiting for me. But I consider my life of no value to myself; my purpose is to finish my course and the ministry I received from the Lord Jesus, to testify to the gospel of God's grace. (Acts 20:22–24)

No one at Ephesus apparently tried to talk Paul out of going to Jerusalem. They were sad because he said that he would not see them again. Setting off on his journey to Jerusalem, Paul went to Tyre, where virtually all the Christians he met were adamant that he should avoid Jerusalem. Luke writes this sobering word:

> Through the Spirit they told Paul not to go to Jerusalem. (21:4)

If we take the view—as I do—that Luke was writing under the inspiration of the Spirit, and since he said that the disciples warned Paul *through the Spirit* that he should not go to Jerusalem, two things might be concluded: (1) the Holy Spirit did not want Paul to go to Jerusalem and, in any case, (2) Luke himself does not think Paul should go to Jerusalem.

This raises all kinds of problems. First, Paul told us not to "despise prophecies" (1 Thess. 5:20). But here he clearly rejected these prophetic words. When Luke refers to Philip having four virgin daughters who prophesied (Acts 21:9), most scholars believe that those prophetic words also warned Paul. Then Agabus appears for the second time in the book of Acts. Luke has already made it clear that Agabus was a true prophet since he predicted "by the Spirit" a forthcoming famine that came to pass (11:27–28). In other words, Luke appears to put the Christians in Tyre and the prophet Agabus in much the same category! Both prophesied in the Spirit. And the same Agabus warned Paul not to go to Jerusalem:

> This is what the Holy Spirit says: "In this way the Jews in Jerusalem will bind the man who owns this belt and deliver him over to the Gentiles." (21:11)

What was going on? It appears that everyone stood against Paul, including Luke! Luke said: "When *we* heard this, both *we* and the local people pleaded with him not to go up to Jerusalem" (v. 12, emphasis mine).

Did Paul accept these prophecies as being from God? Apparently not! Did he consider his status and authority as an apostle superior to these Christians, including Agabus?

Did Paul get out of the will of God by going to Jerusalem?

In this case, Luke tells us that Paul felt "compelled by the Spirit" (20:22).

The bigger question is: Was Luke speaking for God when he said that both these people in Tyre and Agabus prophesied "by the Spirit"? Or was Luke *assuming* that they were predicting "by the Spirit"? As for Agabus's prophecy regarding the famine, he did get that right. But a close look at Agabus's words to Paul regarding going to Jerusalem and being handed over to the Gentiles shows that he did not get that prophecy entirely right! First, the Jews did not bind Paul; the Roman commander did (22:24). Secondly, the Jews did not hand Paul over to the Gentiles; Paul himself *asked* to be tried by Caesar (25:11–12).

Many Bible interpreters have chosen to overlook the details of Agabus and Paul's experience, noting that it was ultimately true that Paul ended up with the Gentiles. But that is not what Agabus said. Then what does it mean that Agabus prophesied "by the Spirit"? My opinion is that Luke was giving Agabus the benefit of the doubt. Here is why I say this: Luke writes that Agabus said, "The Holy Spirit says"—yet Agabus should not have said these words. After all, what he predicted is not what happened. He may have actually also said, "The Holy Spirit says" regarding the famine—and he got that one right. But many good people who have a prophetic gift sometimes assume more than they should! As I show in my book *Prophetic Integrity*, to say the

Spirit "says" or God "says" is misusing God's name to claim that you prophesy by his command!

Even though Agabus heard from God and loved Paul, which was likely why he attempted to prevent Paul from going to Jerusalem, Paul felt just as strong (perhaps stronger) about going. The truth is not that there were competing words from God, but that Paul was willing to go even if he were to be imprisoned, like Agabus said. This fate would seem to be a failure according to Agabus, but it was not for Paul. This is similar to Rebekah's finest hour, when she was willing to be cursed. Paul did not lie or cheat; he knew, however, what it meant to fulfill the word of the Lord. Nobody else saw this, and that is why this was Paul's finest hour—he appeared foolish, even arrogant. He didn't correct his fellow Christians, but went to Jerusalem.

Most of us would likely listen to Agabus. Paul stands out because he cared more about God's glory and mission than his own safety.

Paul knew that God had primarily called him not to convert the Jews but Gentiles (Gal. 2:9). But he had nothing to lose by trying to reach out to his fellow countrymen! He did fail to do this (surprise, surprise). But, as he wrote to the Philippians, "I want you to know, brothers and sisters, that what has happened to me has actually advanced the gospel" (Phil. 1:12). Indeed, many of Paul's epistles were written from a prison in Rome. Where would we be today without Ephesians, Philippians, and Colossians? This is yet more evidence that "all things work together for the good of those who love God, who are called according to his purpose" (Rom. 8:28)!

NINETEEN

Samuel Demonstrating Transparency

Samuel saw Eliab and said [to Jesse], "Certainly the LORD's anointed one is here before him."

But the LORD said to Samuel, "Do not look at his appearance or his stature because I have rejected him. Humans do not see what the LORD sees, for humans see what is visible, but the LORD sees the heart."

. . . Samuel told Jesse, "The LORD hasn't chosen any of these."

—1 Samuel 16:6–7, 10

The greater success a man has made, the more he fears a climb down.

—Lin Yutang (1895–1976)

If spirituality could be defined as closing the time gap between sin and repentance, greatness is closing the time gap between making a mistake and admitting it. Some say, "I'll never admit

I was wrong." Then after some years they say, "Well, I guess I should not have said that." Some close the gap to a few months. Some weeks. Some days. Some hours. Some minutes. Some seconds. We will spare ourselves a lot of grief and embarrassment when we can close the gap to seconds.

The prophet Samuel had a head start. He was the answer to his mother Hannah's prayers and became the promise of her vow to God and the priest Eli. Having been barren for a good while, Hannah vowed to God that if he gave her a son, she would give him to Eli for the work of the Lord. God answered her prayers, and she kept her vow (1 Sam. 1–2). In the days when the word of the Lord was "rare," God unexpectedly spoke directly and clearly to the child Samuel. This shook Eli rigid, but the priest acknowledged that God had truly stepped in to warn that the family of Eli would be eliminated forever owing to its iniquity (1 Sam. 3). Samuel grew up to be the greatest prophet since Moses and became a legend in his time. None of his words "fell to the ground," that is, God "fulfilled everything Samuel prophesied" (3:19). Indeed, all Israel from Dan to Beer-sheba or from north to south knew that Samuel was a "confirmed prophet of the LORD" (vv. 19–21). The people of Israel fully respected Samuel, except for one thing: they asked for a king. They wanted to be like "other nations." Samuel considered their desire wrong, so he prayed to the Lord (8:5–6).

Like many of the people described in this book, many hours could be said to have been Samuel's finest. He showed himself to be a truly great man. In this case, he had to deal with Israel's ill-posed request. He was hurt that Israel insisted on having a king. After all, God was their king. But the Lord told Samuel:

> Listen to the people and everything they say to you. They have not rejected you; they have rejected me as their king. They are doing the same thing to you that they have done to me, since the day I brought them out of Egypt until this day, abandoning me and worshiping other gods. Listen to them, but solemnly warn them and tell them about the customary rights of the king who will reign over them. (vv. 7–9)

Samuel refused to take rejection personally and did not take himself seriously. This, indeed, is a mark of a truly great leader. He was not only a great man of God, but also a great prophet and a wise leader of people. A leader displays weakness when he or she takes rejection personally, even when upholding truth and godly principle. Such leaders fight back at the people who are unhappy with their leadership, rather than letting God handle things. Samuel demonstrated greatness by finding them the best candidate for king he could possibly discover—Saul of the tribe of Benjamin (1 Sam. 9–10).

When King Saul eventually failed as a good king, however, Samuel was patient and did not rub this unfortunate development in Israel's face. After scolding Saul for unlawfully doing the work only a priest was called to do and stating that God would find a man after his own heart (13:8–14), Saul was virtually given a second chance. However, he also blew this opportunity away (1 Sam. 15). As another prophet would say hundreds of years later, "I give you a king in my anger and take away a king in my wrath" (Hos. 13:11).

Another candidate for Samuel's finest hour could have been when he was an old man and was willing to go outside his comfort zone, risking his life by anointing another man king when there already was a king! Acknowledging to Samuel that he had rejected Saul, the Lord asked Samuel to go to the house of Jesse to anoint the next king (1 Sam. 16:1). Showing how human he was, Samuel pleaded with the Lord not to have to do this: "Saul will hear about it and kill me!" (v. 2). One might think that God would give the aged Samuel a break and raise up another prophet to do such dangerous work. But no—God wasn't finished with Samuel yet. Samuel obeyed the Lord to the hilt (vv. 4–5). Nevertheless, I don't think this was his finest hour.

Samuel's last major challenge came when he arrived at the house of Jesse. Possibly wanting to please the father, Jesse, and hastily assuming that Eliab the firstborn would be God's obvious choice, Samuel jumped the gun. He let Jesse and seven men—all hoping to be tapped—know that he had picked Eliab. Yes, the great Samuel had quickly chosen Eliab! Whoops! The Lord intervened and said to Samuel:

> Humans do not see what the Lord sees, for humans see what is visible, but the Lord sees the heart. (v. 7)

Now, in front of Jesse and seven men, Samuel climbs down. He admits he got it wrong. Oh, that prophetic men and women would learn from the humble Samuel! As Lin Yutang the Chinese inventor and author put it—having converted from Christianity to Buddhism and back to Christianity—"The greater success a man has made, the more he fears a climb down."

But there is no sign that Samuel was embarrassed by his mistake. He just proceeded to find the right man—from Abinadab to Shammah to all seven present. He is more careful this time, but it looks like his visit to Jesse's house has come to nothing.

"The LORD hasn't chosen any of these," Samuel has to tell Jesse. "Are these all the sons you have?" (v. 10–11).

Jesse replied (in so many words): "No. But you surely won't want him because he is the youngest and he is tending the sheep."

"Send for him," orders the great prophet, realizing he hasn't messed up this time.

In comes the teenager David, the last person anyone—including his father—expected to be chosen as the next king (vv. 11–12).

Since Samuel served God and Israel with such a great anointing, it is difficult to narrow in on his finest hour. Yes, Samuel took his prophetic role seriously and his anointing was unquestioned. He served God and Israel before his own desires. And, collectively, you could say that all three of the stories I have presented were his finest hour. But at the peak of his life and ministry, the prophet humbly admits in the company of Jesse and his older sons that he got it wrong. In combination with humility and discerning God's chosen king, Samuel had his finest hour. At his ego's expense, Samuel's finest hour was identifying David as the one nobody would have dreamed would be future king of Israel.

This was Samuel's finest hour and David's defining moment.

TWENTY

Peter, John, and Second Chances

After they called in the apostles and had them flogged, they ordered them not to speak in the name of Jesus and released them. Then they went out from the presence of the Sanhedrin, rejoicing that they were counted worthy to be treated shamefully on behalf of the Name.

—Acts 5:40–41

I loved the garish day, and, in spite of fears,
Pride ruled my will: remember not past years.

—John Henry Newman (1801–1890)

A second look He gave, which said,
"I freely all forgive;
This blood is for thy ransom paid;
I die that thou mayest live."

—John Newton (1725–1807)

Peter and John go back a long way. They were close friends; both were businessmen and Galilean fishermen. As we will see soon, there may have been a benign rivalry between them, especially in Peter's eyes. The two men were discovered by Jesus and called to be fishers of "people" at much the same time (Matt. 4:18–22).

The Gospels present Peter as the most colorful follower of Jesus; an extrovert and ever the vocal one and the most sure of himself. Peter was the first to affirm Jesus as the Messiah, the Son of God (16:16), but was rebuked by Jesus soon afterward for being a "hindrance" by thinking of his own selfish concerns more than God's concerns (v. 23). Peter also thought that he was doing a valiant thing on the Mount of Transfiguration by suggesting that they set up three shelters—one for Jesus, one for Moses, and one for Elijah (17:4).

Peter sincerely thought that he loved Jesus more than the other disciples did. When Jesus attempted to wash Peter's feet, Peter piously said: "You will never wash my feet." Then Jesus replied, "If I don't wash you, you have no part with me," whereupon Peter retorted, "Lord, not only my feet, but also my hands and my head" (John 13:8–9).

Peter wanted to outdo the other disciples in showing fidelity to Jesus. In reply, Jesus said to him: "Look out. Satan has asked to sift you like wheat. But I have prayed for you that your faith may not fail. And you, when you have turned back, strengthen your brothers." Peter then wanted to assure Jesus: "I'm ready to go with you both to prison and to death" (Luke 22:31–33).

At another time, Peter declared, "I will lay down my life for you" (John 13:37). But Jesus, not only knowing what was going to happen in the next few hours but, in any case, always knowing "what was in man" (2:25), replied to Peter, "Will you lay down your life for me? Truly I tell you, a rooster will not crow until you have denied me three times" (13:38).

Peter, along with James and John, was in Jesus's inner circle. These three men were chosen to be present at the healing of Jairus's daughter (Luke 8:49–56), at the Mount of Transfiguration when Jesus's glory was manifested (Matt. 17:1–8), and in Gethsemane when Jesus pleaded with the Father to avoid the crucifixion, if at all possible (26:37–39). In the garden, Jesus singled out Peter to share his disappointment: "So, couldn't you stay awake with me one hour?" (v. 40). Nevertheless, Peter and the others all fell asleep again.

As for Peter denying Jesus, Peter thought there was no way under the sun such a thing could happen. While he was warming himself near a fire outside the high priest's courtyard, only hours after Jesus's arrest, a servant girl approached Peter and said, "You were with Jesus the Galilean too."

Nonsense, said Peter. "I don't know what you're talking about."

Then another woman saw Peter and said, "This man was with Jesus the Nazarene!"

This time Peter swore with an oath: "I don't know the man!"

After a little while later, with Jesus watching, some other people approached and said to Peter, "You really are one of them, since even your accent gives you away."

At this point Peter began to curse and swear with an oath, "I don't know the man!" (vv. 69–75).

Immediately a rooster crowed. "Then the Lord turned and looked at Peter. So Peter remembered the word of the Lord, how he had said to him, 'Before the rooster crows today, you will deny me three times.' And he went outside and wept bitterly" (Luke 22:61–62).

That was Peter's worst moment. There is no way anyone could clearly convey the sense of grief and guilt Peter felt at that moment. He would have given anything—anything—to turn the clock back or, at least, to have a second chance to show how he felt about Jesus.

In contrast to Peter, John appears to be the quieter man and more introverted. I believe he authored the Gospel of John, the three epistles attributed to him, and the book of Revelation. While John was not portrayed as vocally denying Jesus, Matthew says of the Twelve, implying also Judas Iscariot's betrayal: "all the disciples deserted him and ran away" (Matt. 26:56). John too, then, could never forget that he also had forsaken his Lord. He also would welcome any opportunity to show that he had been granted repentance for siding with the other disciples rather than supporting Jesus.

Reader, have you ever wished for a second chance? Do you know what it is like to have messed up? Would you give a thousand worlds for God to turn the clock back?

Be of good cheer: the God of the Bible is the God of the second chance. Or, better still, he is a God who forgives our past as if it did not exist!

After his resurrection from the dead, Jesus walked through closed doors, showing up in a room with ten guilty and fearful disciples. Instead of throwing the book at them for deserting him in his suffering, Jesus said, "Peace be with you." There was no need to worry. Moreover, "As the Father has sent me, I also send you" (John 20:21).

Amazing! It was as though nothing had happened to disrupt the disciples' relationship with Jesus or the Father's purpose. What grace! What mercy! Indescribable. Overwhelming. But should this be so surprising? After all, Jesus had said to Peter, "I have prayed for you." Not only that, but he also had told Peter, "A rooster will not crow until you have denied me three times. Don't let your heart be troubled. Believe in God; believe also in me" (13:38–14:1).

Some time later, Jesus asked Peter: "Do you love me more than these?" (21:15). I believe Jesus was referring to the other disciples when he said "more than these" (that is, "Do you love me more than these other disciples do?"). Peter insisted that he did. Then Jesus spoke another prophetic word to Peter:

> Truly I tell you, when you were younger, you would tie your belt and walk wherever you wanted. But when you grow old, you will stretch out your hands and someone else will tie you and carry you where you don't want to go. (v. 18)

Jesus was indicating by what kind of death Peter would "glorify God" (v. 19). But, in response, Peter wanted to know what would happen to John, who was following them at that moment. Jesus replied, "What is that to you? As for you, follow me" (v. 22).

Until now my focus has been on Peter. The Gospel writers focused on him more than John. Nevertheless, John, along with the rest of the disciples, also denied Jesus. It is true that we don't see him denying Jesus as much as Peter. But after the resurrection John is willing to be identified with Peter, and they are linked together in the book of Acts.

Peter preached the inaugural sermon of the church on the

day of Pentecost, and he and John were instrumental at the Beautiful Gate in the healing of the forty-year-old man who had never walked (Acts 3). Consequently, they got in trouble with the Sanhedrin for the miracle and were summoned to appear before them.

The Sanhedrin regarded themselves as the ultimate authority to carry out the Mosaic law in Israel. They took themselves very seriously. Made up of Pharisees and Sadducees, they were eager to put Peter and John on the spot. However, one of their prominent members, Gamaliel, urged his colleagues to be careful what they did to Peter and John—lest they unwittingly be found fighting against God (5:39). His counsel kept the Sanhedrin from ordering the deaths of Peter and John then and there. Instead, they had the apostles flogged and warned them not to speak in the name of Jesus.

Peter and John would have gladly welcomed death, and could not believe their luck—that they were "counted worthy to be treated shamefully on behalf of the Name" (v. 41)! They had deserted Jesus for fear of their reputation, and now they had been given a second chance. This time, Peter and John did not care about their reputation. All this felt too good to be true! While the Pharisees and Sadducees sat around gloating that they had taught these men a lesson, they could not have known that they had just given Peter and John their finest hour.

TWENTY-ONE

Abraham's Faith When God Didn't Make Sense

God tested Abraham and said to him, "Abraham!"

"Here I am," he answered.

"Take your son," he said, "your only son Isaac, whom you love, go to the land of Moriah, and offer him there as a burnt offering on one of the mountains I will tell you about" . . .

When they arrived at the place that God had told him about, Abraham built the altar there and arranged the wood. He bound his son Isaac and placed him on the altar on top of the wood. Then Abraham reached out and took the knife to slaughter his son.

But the angel of the LORD called to him from heaven and said, "Abraham, Abraham!"

He replied, "Here I am."

Then he said, "Do not lay a hand on the boy or do anything to him. For now I know that you fear God, since you have not withheld your only son from me." . . .

Then the angel of the LORD called to Abraham a second time from heaven and said, "By myself I have sworn," this is the LORD's declaration: "Because you have done this thing and have not withheld your only son, I will indeed bless you and make your offspring as numerous as the stars of the sky and the sand on the seashore."

—Genesis 22:1–2, 9–12, 15–17

Nowhere in the Bible does God speak defensively or seek our approval on His matters. He simply says, "Trust Me."

—James Dobson

No servant of God in the Bible had more to complain about than Abraham. He was promised the land of Canaan for an inheritance, but when he went out he "did not know where he was going" (Heb. 11:8). Not only that, when Abraham came into the promised land God "didn't give him an inheritance in it—not even a foot of ground" (Acts 7:5). Figure that out! John Calvin observed that Abraham must surely have felt deceived or betrayed. In a word: Abraham, more than any character in Holy Scripture, must head the list of those who felt that God made no sense!

Yet more difficulties followed. When Abraham was about eighty-five and his wife Sarah was seventy-five, God promised him a son from his own body. Since Sarah was now barren, this surely made no sense! But Abraham believed God's promise and his faith was counted for righteousness (Gen. 15:6), this being Paul's chief illustration for the teaching of justification by faith alone.

But there is still more to tell! When Sarah didn't get pregnant, she persuaded Abraham to make good God's promise by sleeping with her servant Hagar (Gen. 16). Abraham, therefore, assumed that when Hagar conceived and had the male child Ishmael, this must have been what God had in mind all along. Wrong! God revealed to Abraham and Sarah that *she would conceive after all*—that Isaac was coming and that Isaac, not Ishmael, was the child of promise. Can you blame Abraham for being confused?

I had a vivid supernatural experience on October 31, 1955. What I saw was more real to me than anything I ever saw with my physical eyes or heard with my physical ears. I was driving on old U.S. 41 in Tennessee between Monteagle and Nashville. Suddenly, Jesus appeared before me, praying for me. I felt overwhelmed. I was fascinated that he was positioned at the right hand of the Father. I could not tell what Jesus was saying, but never in my lifetime—before or since—had I felt so loved. I wept and watched. I do not know how I drove for the next eighty miles.

Over an hour later, as I passed through Smyrna, I distinctly heard Jesus say to the Father, "He wants it." I heard the Father reply, "He can have it." At that precise moment I felt a warmth in my chest and a peace and joy in my heart that surpassed anything I have ever—ever—felt. I saw the physical face of Jesus for about a minute. Then it diminished. I had no idea at that time what had happened to me. It all made no sense.

What I do know is that my theology underwent a major surgery—I would call it a personal paradigm shift. By sundown that very day, I had learned two indisputable things from this experience: (1) I was eternally and unconditionally saved (which went completely against everything I had been taught); and (2) I was sovereignly chosen (which I had known nothing about). For days I wondered (I am almost ashamed to say) if I was the only person to have this kind of experience. Had I come to believe something new?

My memory and details of that experience are as real today as if it had happened yesterday. This vision is more real than the Nashville skyline Louise and I see from our condo every day. Ironically, we now live on U.S. 41 in Nashville, overlooking Nissan Stadium, where the Titans play. But it took a long time—years—before I could say what Jesus's words "He wants it . . . he can have it" meant. I now know that "it" is the *oath* as described in Hebrews 6:16–17, where the writer says that the "oath ends every dispute." Hebrews 6:18 also refers to "two unchangeable things," i.e., the promise and the oath. Finally, the author calls "it" the "rest" in Hebrews 4:1 and 4:10.

The "oath" is called by other names in the Bible: "the rest," "inheritance," and "full assurance." The Westminster Confession also refers to "infallible assurance" not belonging to the "essence of faith." I take this to mean that you can be a good Christian without experiencing unbroken assurance. This type of assurance comes pretty close—I think—as a fulfilling reward to those who don't give up even during a season in which God seems to make no sense. It is a reward worth waiting for.

Let's get back to Abraham and his greatest challenge.

> Take your son, your only son Isaac, whom you love, go to the land of Moriah, and offer him there as a burnt offering on one of the mountains I will tell you about. (Gen. 22:2)

I find it impossible to put myself in Abraham's shoes in this moment. How did Abraham's trust in God—what did he see or feel?—give him the willingness to sacrifice Isaac? Abraham's actions recorded for us in Scripture have been questioned and commented on for ages. We only know that he did what God told him to do.

Risking everything that was promised to him, Abraham could not have known what would follow. Nobody was there to witness his actions—God alone was his witness.

Nevertheless, Abraham obeyed. And that was his finest hour.

What followed Abraham's finest hour was a big deal. The writer of Hebrews wants us to know just how big a deal it was for God to swear an oath to Abraham. Whereas one swears an oath by something "greater"—whether it be by the Holy Bible or something that seems sacred (one may say, "I swear by my mother's grave")—God could not find anything greater. Therefore, he swore "by himself" (Heb. 6:13):

> I will indeed bless you and make your offspring as numerous as the stars of the sky and the sand on the seashore. Your offspring will possess the city gates of their enemies. And all the nations of the earth will be blessed by your offspring because you have obeyed my command. (Gen. 22:17–18)

The letter to the Hebrews refers to Abraham having experienced God's oath. The oath came to him after he became utterly willing—indeed, he was in the process of sacrificing Isaac as a burnt offering. Receiving God's oath was Abraham's reward for his obedience.

The moment when God swore an oath to Abraham was ten thousand times more powerful to Abraham than my experience on U.S. 41 was to myself. Furthermore, Abraham was over one hundred years old, but I was only nineteen—which I find embarrassing to say (if I am totally honest). Why did God give *me* this vision? I honestly do not know. But I do know one thing for sure: I had done nothing before, nor have I done anything ever since to deserve this blessing. At the same time, the experience of God swearing an oath is promised to ALL believers, and this blessing has happened to millions all over the world.

Abraham would never ever doubt God's promise again. Had he doubted God's word before the oath came? Possibly. From Genesis 12 through Genesis 21, God spoke at different times to Abraham—again and again. But he only spoke by promise—promise after promise. Finally, for the first time in Abraham's life, God swore an oath to him. What does this mean? Answer: the oath ends all dispute. An oath is more convincing than a promise. Whereas both a promise from God and an oath from God are equally true, the oath removes all doubt. After God swore an oath to Abraham, you could say that he was "set." Never again would Abraham need more convincing—the oath did it. Nothing, indeed, tops experience over argument. It is like seeing the Swiss Alps rather than viewing pictures of them.

Times will come in your life when God doesn't make sense. You probably already have had some of those experiences. But I want to encourage you that in those times you can believe God even more. Let Abraham be our guide into believing that God's promises are worth trusting even in the midst of confusing times.

TWENTY-TWO

Samson and All's Well That Ends Well

Samson said, "Let me die with the Philistines." He pushed with all his might, and the temple fell on the leaders and all the people in it. And those he killed at his death were more than those he had killed in his life.

—Judges 16:30

That strength which he had lost by sin, he recovers by prayer. That it was not from passion or personal revenge, but from holy zeal for the glory of God and Israel, appears from God accepting and answering the prayer. The house was pulled down, not from the natural strength of Samson, but by the almighty power of God.

—Matthew Henry (1662–1714)

Some of the people named in Hebrews 11 surprise me. Were you surprised to learn that Samson, who is often referred to as the strongest man in the world but arguably is actually the weakest, has a place in Hebrews 11? Why does Jephthah have a place in this list, despite his foolish vow (v. 32)? Also, who would have guessed that Peter would refer to Lot as a "righteous" man (2 Peter 2:7)? Furthermore, as we saw earlier, what about King David—an adulterer and murderer—who was described as a "man after God's own heart" (cf. 1 Sam. 13:14; Acts 13:22)?

First, I believe that God is kinder and more gracious than you and I are.

David had learned this truth about God when the prophet Gad offered him choices of punishment for his folly of numbering the people:

> I'm in anguish. Please, let me fall into the LORD's hands because his mercies are very great, but don't let me fall into human hands. (1 Chron. 21:13)

Also, secondly, God thinks differently than we do:

> "For my thoughts are not your thoughts,
> and your ways are not my ways."
> This is the LORD's declaration.
> "For as heaven is higher than earth,
> so my ways are higher than your ways,
> and my thoughts than your thoughts."
> (Isa. 55:8–9)

It hardly needs to be stated that there is something reprehensible in every saint, and Samson is no exception. But God clearly sought after and chose him (Judg. 13:24–25). The Spirit bestowed tremendous physical strength upon him as a gift. He was similar to Superman or Captain Marvel, whom I used to read about in comics books as a boy. However, Samson's gift did not appear to help him overcome his weakness, which was a fondness for women. To be honest, many leaders suffer from this flaw. Billy Graham once noted, "It seems that the devil seems to get seventy-five percent of God's best servants through sexual temptation." I believe this is true. When I hear of a fellow minister who falls because of sexual sin, I have to say in my heart, "That's me."

What really astounds me is how many powerful preachers are able to continue in ministry with great effectiveness while also carrying on a secret affair the entire time. When I was a teenager, one of my early heroes came yearly to our church in Ashland, Kentucky. He was a popular evangelist with exceptional power, preaching with great persuasiveness that God used to convert many people night after night. However, I later found out that a woman had followed him all over America, booking into the same hotel in the town where he was conducting a "revival." Our pastor discovered this unusual circumstance while the evangelist was at our church, but he did not confront him until after the evangelist had preached his final scheduled message. How should I explain the incongruity between this preacher's powerful ministry and his secret sin? In reply, I point out that King Saul did prophesy on his way to kill David (1 Sam. 19:23–24) and that the gifts are irrevocable (Rom. 11:29—"without repentance" KJV).

It is also true that many people who appear to be spiritual, godly, powerful, and anointed are successful in what they do, but are also shockingly weak in sexual discipline.

Why do so many spiritual leaders struggle with this sin? Is

it because they have a stronger sexual appetite than others? Or do they have greater egos and desire to impress the people they like? When James warned that the tongue is a "fire" and that a spark could set a forest on fire (James 3:5), it appears that he was referring to those who can't seem to resist saying anything flattering and end up breaking up a marriage or losing a job.

My father used to say to me, "Son, the devil is crafty." But *the human heart* is also deceitful and desperately wicked (Jer. 17:9). This is why Solomon said, "Keep thy heart with all diligence; for out of it are the issues of life" (Prov. 4:23 KJV). There is simply no doctrine or practice of sanctification that eradicates our minds from temptation. I'm sorry, but I don't agree that the line "temptations lose their power when Thou art nigh" in the great hymn "I need Thee Every Hour" is always true. Sometimes, yes. But not always. This is why Paul pleads for us to see sanctification as a progressive work. Sanctification isn't easy—indeed, it is very often hard work! But the reward is worth working for:

> Get wisdom, get understanding;
> don't forget or turn away from the words from
> my mouth.
> Don't abandon wisdom, and she will watch
> over you;
> love her, and she will guard you.
> Wisdom is supreme—so get wisdom.
> And whatever else you get, get understanding.
> Cherish her, and she will exalt you;
> if you embrace her, she will honor you.
> She will place a garland of favor on your head;
> she will give you a crown of beauty. (vv. 5–9)

The book of Proverbs goes on and on about the importance of sexual purity (especially chapters 5 and 7). It repeatedly warns you to your face that wisdom and sexual purity go together; that giving into sexual temptation outside of marriage kisses wisdom good-bye. To repeat: wisdom and sexual sin do not go together! Those who have true wisdom are those who have not only learned but keep resisting sexual temptation. I personally do not think that ministers, preachers, pastors, bishops, and evangelists can emphasize this truth too strongly! How can powerful, talented, and famed church leaders lose their ministries overnight from sexual sin? Answer: lack of wisdom.

The strongest man in the world had to know that Delilah was not a true friend. Why did Samson let her keep asking him for his secret when she was obviously on the side of the Philistines and not Israel (Judg. 16:4–15)? Yet he clearly continued to lay his head on her lap. But one day Samson gave into Delilah's nagging. She wore him out with her accusations that he did not love her. Why would Samson ever want Delilah to think that he loved her? Samson simply wanted sex, but in order to get Delilah to give him her body he seemed to think he needed to convince her that he loved her. His love was not pure; it was sensual, physical love.

One of the saddest lines in all Holy Writ is when Samson said to Delilah, "My hair has never been cut, because I am a Nazirite to God from birth. If I am shaved, my strength will leave me, and I will become weak and be like any other man" (v. 17). This time Delilah knew that Samson was telling her the truth. She did not have the slightest feeling of love for him—could he not see that? But *eros* love can be so blinding.

Samson seemingly had no willpower to resist Delilah a minute longer. He gave in. "She let him fall asleep on her lap and called a man to shave off the seven braids on his head. In this way, she made him helpless, and his strength left him" (v. 19). When Samson woke up and was challenged, "he did not know that the LORD had left him" (v. 20). Surprise, surprise—he was as weak as a kitten.

What fascinates me is how Samson did not feel a loss of power—he did not feel a thing—after he woke up with a shorn head. This is typical of sin; one can do horrible things and feel nothing. No conscience. No conviction. No shame. This is what often happens when a Christian grieves the Holy Spirit. As the backslider is filled with his own ways (Prov. 14:14 KJV) whether he loses his temper, speaks evil of another, or gives into sexual temptation, so does the backsliding Christian feel nothing which should be a warning shout to him. But, like Samson, who thought he was as strong as ever, such a Christian will immediately discover that he is as weak as any human being! Consequently, the Philistines wasted no time getting vengeance on their enemy number one:

> The Philistines seized him and gouged out his eyes. They brought him down to Gaza and bound him with bronze shackles, and he was forced to grind grain in the prison. (Judg. 16:21)

The "secret of the LORD is with them that fear him" (Ps. 25:14 KJV). Many versions of Psalm 25:14 say that the Lord "confides" in those who fear him. Whatever version you prefer, the question is: Do you value an intimate relationship with the Lord? Can he confide in you without your sharing such a secret with the world—or even with your best friend? If God trusts you with a secret that is meant to be kept between him and you, you should guard it as though it were worth a billion dollars in gold. For such wisdom is what Proverbs is setting before our eyes. Go for it, settle for nothing less, get it—whatever the cost!

In this manner, God was extremely kind to Samson. There was one item that the Philistines had not counted on:

> [Samson's] hair began to grow back after it had been shaved. (Judg. 16:22)

Samson knew that his hair began to grow again. He would not get his eyesight back—his hair growing back would not erase the past. But it meant that his old anointing was being restored, and he knew what this meant. The enemy did not know God's ways. The pitiful Samson, now blind forever, asked God to give him one more chance to show how much he truly loved God. In the temple of Dagon, Samson asked for help from a boy who was leading him by the hand, saying to him:

> Lead me where I can feel the pillars supporting the temple, so I can lean against them. (v. 26)

The temple was full, all the leaders of the Philistines were there, and about three thousand men and women were on the roof laughing at Samson as he entertained them.

During this moment, Samson's finest hour finally came even in the midst of his outward humiliation. Here is the scene in full detail:

> [Samson] called out to the LORD, "Lord GOD, please remember me. Strengthen me, God, just once more. With one act of vengeance, let me pay back the Philistines for my two eyes." Samson took hold of the two middle pillars supporting the temple and leaned against them, one on his right hand and the other on his left. Samson said, "Let me die with the Philistines." He pushed with all his might, and the temple fell on the leaders and all the people in it. And those he killed at his death were more than those he had killed in his life. (vv. 28–30)

Did Samson deserve to have a good ending? No. Do any of us deserve to have all things work together for good (Rom. 8:28)? Hardly. But we serve a gracious God who delights in showing mercy to the most unworthy—that is, to those who *feel* the most unworthy. You can be sure that this was exactly the way Samson felt. And God came through for him.

TWENTY-THREE

Daniel and the Three Hebrews' *But-If-Not* Faith

Shadrach, Meshach, and Abednego replied to the king, "Nebuchadnezzar, we don't need to give you an answer to this question. If the God we serve exists, then he can rescue us from the furnace of blazing fire, and he can rescue us from the power of you, the king. But even if he does not rescue us, we want you as king to know that we will not serve your gods or worship the gold statue you set up."

—Daniel 3:16–18

When Daniel learned that the document had been signed, he went into his house. The windows in its upstairs room opened toward Jerusalem, and three times a day he got down on his knees, prayed, and gave thanks to his God, just as he had done before.

—Daniel 6:10

Richard Wurmbrand (1909–2001), author of *Tortured for Christ*, wrote about witnessing to inmates in a Romanian prison that was under Communist control:

> It was strictly forbidden to preach to other prisoners, as it is in captive nations today. It was understood that whoever was caught doing this received a severe beating. A number of us decided to pay the price for the privilege of preaching, so we accepted their terms. It was a deal: we preached and they beat us. We were happy preaching; they were happy beating us—so everyone was happy. (p. 58 of the 50th anniversary edition, 2017)

The absurdity of the final sentence made me burst out in laughter for several minutes when I first read it. It still makes me laugh today.

I did meet Wurmbrand some fifty years ago when I was a seminary student. I asked him for his wisdom on a matter, and his reply was: "Young man, spend more time talking to God about men than talking to men about God." I never had received advice like that before—or ever have since. He was a rare breed. I have no doubt that he was as bold as Daniel and the three Hebrews in Babylon.

We saw earlier how Jeremiah was accused of treason for prophesying that Israel would be carried captive to Babylon. Jeremiah was vindicated because that day did come. Daniel and the three young Hebrew men were among those who were forced to go and live in Babylon. Their first major test after they arrived was if they would eat the king's food against their convictions, and they resolved that they would not defile themselves this way (Dan. 1:8). The four young men agreed to be tested by letting the Babylonian authorities examine them after ten days on their chosen diet. They were vindicated, being found to be healthier than the other men (v. 15). Furthermore, they were ten times better in wisdom and understanding than any of the magicians and mediums in the entire kingdom (v. 20).

A greater challenge came when King Nebuchadnezzar made a gold statue ninety feet high and nine feet wide, which all were required to worship:

> A herald loudly proclaimed, "People of every nation and language, you are commanded: When you hear the sound of the horn, flute, zither, lyre, harp, drum, and every kind of music, you are to fall facedown and worship the gold statue that King Nebuchadnezzar has set up. But whoever does not fall down and worship will immediately be thrown into a furnace of blazing fire." (3:4–6)

Everyone fell down and worshiped. When Shadrach, Meshach, and Abednego were discovered not observing the king's command, they were summoned before Nebuchadnezzar. He reprimanded, rebuked, and warned them:

> If you don't worship it, you will immediately be thrown into a furnace of blazing fire—and who is the god who can rescue you from my power? (v. 15)

Then came the historic answer from the three Hebrews:

> Nebuchadnezzar, we don't need to give you an answer to this question. If the God we serve exists, then he can rescue us from the furnace of blazing fire, and he can rescue us from the power of you, the king. But even if he does not rescue us, we want you as king to know that we will not serve your gods or worship the gold statue you set up. (vv. 16–18)

The King James Version uses a peculiar phrase that has stuck with me over the years:

> But if not, be it known unto thee, O king, that we will not serve thy gods, nor worship the golden image which thou hast set up.

Some seventy years ago, at a Wednesday night prayer meeting attended by a dozen people in a home in Birmingham, Alabama, a sweet lady challenged all present with the following question:

> Do you have the "but if not" faith?

I have thought of this question a thousand times. Were you and I, reader, to manifest the answer to this question in our darkest hour, it would also be our finest hour.

Many readers will know how this scenario ended. The king went to observe the three Hebrews in the searingly hot, fiery furnace.

> [Nebuchadnezzar] said to his advisors, "Didn't we throw three men, bound, into the fire?"

> "Yes, of course, Your Majesty," they replied to the king.
>
> He exclaimed, "Look! I see four men, not tied, walking around in the fire unharmed; and the fourth looks like a son of the gods." (vv. 24–25)

My dad used to tell me the story of the three Hebrew children—as well as stories about most of the characters of the book of Daniel—when I was a boy. He would end the story of the three Hebrews by asking me, "What burned in the fiery furnace?" The answer, of course: "the rope."

Sometime later Daniel was made an administrator in the kingdom of Darius, who had conquered Babylon for the Persian Empire. Daniel distinguished himself above all the rest of the administrators and satraps, having "an extraordinary spirit" (6:3), so the king planned to set him over the whole realm. But these other officials were jealous of Daniel. They wanted to get him removed from his position, but they knew that this was unlikely unless they could "find something against him concerning the law of his God" (v. 5). The officials went to the king and made the following suggestion:

> The king should establish an ordinance and enforce an edict that, for thirty days, anyone who petitions any god or man except you, the king, will be thrown into the lions' den. Therefore, Your Majesty, establish the edict and sign the document so that, as a law of the Medes and Persians, it is irrevocable and cannot be changed. (vv. 7b–8)

Here was Daniel's response:

> When Daniel learned that the document had been signed, he went into his house. The windows in the upstairs room opened toward Jerusalem, and three times a day he got down on his knees, prayed, and gave thanks to his God, just as he had done before. (v. 10)

Daniel's jealous enemies wasted no time. They quickly reminded Darius of this new edict.

> The king answered, "As a law of the Medes and Persians, the order stands and is irrevocable."
>
> Then they replied to the king, "Daniel, one of the Judean exiles, has ignored you, the king, and the edict you signed, for he prays three times a day." (vv. 12b–13)

Darius was not happy to hear this news! He accordingly set his mind on rescuing Daniel, making every effort to save him. But these same men reminded the king: "You know, Your Majesty, that it is a law of the Medes and Persians that no edict or ordinance the king establishes can be changed" (v. 15).

Daniel was then thrown into the lions' den, the king resigning his fate to God: "May your God, whom you continually serve, rescue you!" (v. 16). Darius spent a sleepless night, and promptly rushed to the den at daybreak, deeply anguished.

> "Daniel, servant of the living God," the king said, "has your God, whom you continually serve, been able to rescue you from the lions?"
>
> Then Daniel spoke with the king: "May the king live

> forever. My God sent his angel and shut the lions' mouths; and they haven't harmed me." (vv. 20–22)

In the cases of both Daniel and the three Hebrews, we learn about their *but if not* faith. In both cases, their lives were on the line: either God would deliver them, or they would suffer. These instances were their finest hours. Without knowing the outcome of their actions, all four men sought the glory of God alone. God does not always deliver you from injustice—I believe Daniel and the three Hebrews understood this. They knew they were not invincible, yet their *but if not* faith in God was stronger than assimilation. In the end, the three Hebrews' lives were preserved in the fire, even though the men who threw them in perished. And King Darius had the men who accused Daniel thrown into the lions' den—along with their families (all perished). Additionally, both Nebuchadnezzar and Darius openly declared that the God of these four Hebrews be regarded as the true living God, whose kingdom would never be destroyed (3:28–29; 6:25–27).

One final comment: if you and I are to have the "but if not" faith, we should be ready when our potential finest hour is set before us.

TWENTY-FOUR

Ruth and Costly Loyalty

Don't plead with me to abandon you
or to return and not follow you.
For wherever you go, I will go,
and wherever you live, I will live;
your people will be my people,
and your God will be my God.
Where you die, I will die,
and there I will be buried.
May the LORD *punish me,*
and do so severely,
if anything but death separates you and me.

—Ruth 1:16–17

Where the battle rages, there the loyalty of the soldier is proved.

—Martin Luther (1483–1546)

I'm for him, right or wrong.

—My grandpa McCurley (1890–1959)

Only two women in history have a book in the Bible named after them—Esther (who was Jewish) and Ruth (a Moabite). Whereas Esther shared her glory with Mordecai, Ruth's voluntary commitment to Naomi stands by itself. Indeed, her decision to stay with Naomi fits my definition of "finest hour" as beautifully as anyone else in this book. You will recall that I choose to see a person's "finest hour" as a moment when he or she is self-effacing and forfeits any glory from people. Ruth had nothing to gain and everything to lose by her decision to follow Naomi. But we will see in this chapter that she not only was eventually rewarded with a family of her own, but would receive posthumous glory by being a part of the lineage of God's Messiah (Matt. 1:5)!

I have had reason to be gripped by the word "loyalty" for most of my life. You will recall my experience of the Holy Spirit which happened on October 31, 1955. Thrilling and life-changing though this was, it led to facing disloyalty again and again and again. It first led to my eventual break with my old denomination, but especially with my father. These were extremely hard days. My father said I had broken with God. My family—grandparents, aunts, and uncles—were not sure what to think. I heard later that at a dinner table they had a heavy discussion with my relatives on my mother's side. All were Nazarenes and were very upset about what appeared to mean my eventual departure from that denomination. However, I learned secondhand that my grandpa McCurley had spoken up with a comment that ended the discussion. Referring to me, he said: "I'm for him, right or wrong."

This statement by my maternal grandfather was the most

loving, the most affirming, the most encouraging, and the most loyal word I have ever received from anybody in my entire lifetime.

When it comes to loyalty, it doesn't get any better than that!

I could not have known in those difficult days that being rejected by my dad—although this was temporary—was a drop in the bucket when compared to what I would face later on. Perhaps one day I will have the liberty to share more, I can only say now that my last sixty years have included experience after experience of being wounded by disloyalty. Whether the reason has been my new theology, my difficult personality, or having "bad luck" with my mentors or my closest friends, these difficult experiences have helped me develop some thoughts about loyalty. For one thing, there is no way you can predict accurately whether a person will be loyal. There are no personality tests, no IQ tests, and no set of interviews containing every question under the sun or references from people who intimately know the person you are about to be associated with that can tell you whether that individual will be loyal. I had four mentors—two betrayed me. I had five assistants during my twenty-five years at Westminster—three were loyal. I have had a dozen close friends—most of them remained loyal friends. But some who suddenly distanced themselves from me were men whom I would never have dreamed would do this.

I have come to accept that most people we have to forgive do not think they have done anything wrong at all!

These things said, there are likely people out there who believe that I did betray them! I think of the famous remark made by Prime Minister Margaret Thatcher (1925–2013) when she felt betrayed by a man who had been a loyal conservative friend: "It's a funny old world."

My point is this: loyalty is an unpredictable trait. Even though I have often observed, "Every person I began to admire a little bit too much sooner or later disappointed me," I should not have been surprised. After all, the heart is "more deceitful than anything else, and incurable—who can understand it?" (Jer. 17:9). My heart is no exception.

That said, my coming to embrace total forgiveness has been precipitated by being betrayed. The disloyalty of others has actually been my salvation! I cannot thank God enough for every single person who betrayed me. But I also admit that I have found disloyalty the hardest thing to forgive, especially when considering J. R. R. Tolkien's (1892–1973) shrewd observation, "Faithless is he who says farewell when the road darkens."

What makes it difficult to forgive is when you suspect that a person's betrayal was almost certainly rooted in self-protection. This happens all too often when the road darkens.

You can possibly now see how I cherish my grandfather's word, "I'm for him, right or wrong." The only other person I can think of who is like this is . . . Jesus.

Ruth is so remarkable because she made her memorable comment at the beginning of her new journey. The question we could ask, then, is: Did Ruth *maintain* such a commitment?

The story begins with Naomi, a widow with two daughters-in-law, Ruth and Orpah. Naomi decided to return to her native Bethlehem. Ruth and Orpah at first decided to follow Naomi but Naomi pleaded with Ruth and Orpah to stay in their native Moab:

> Return home, my daughters. Why do you want to go with me? Am I able to have any more sons who could become your husbands? Return home, my daughters. Go on, for I am too

> old to have another husband. Even if I thought there were still hope for me to have a husband tonight and to bear sons, would you be willing to wait for them to grow up? Would you restrain yourselves from remarrying? No, my daughters, my life is too bitter for you to share, because the LORD's hand has turned against me. (Ruth 1:11–13)

Orpah then decided to stay with her family and friends in Moab, but Ruth "clung" to Naomi. She said:

> Don't plead with me to abandon you
> or to return and not follow you.
> For wherever you go, I will go . . .
> *your God will be my God.*" (v. 16, emphasis mine)

One could say that only Abraham showed such a radical change. Abraham became willing to leave his family, his country, and a pagan religion (Gen. 12:1). Ruth knew that Naomi was an Israelite. Ruth would not only be saying goodbye to her family and her native homeland Moab, but she knew she would be in a different religious world where there was reverence for a personal God and his laws. This was Ruth's decision to convert to the true God. Indeed, her pledge to Naomi showed that she had already been converted in her heart! This, in fact, was the secret to Ruth's loyalty: a heart change had already occurred.

This brings to mind the most spectacular conversion of my ministry. A Muslim woman named Miah approached me following a Friday night Bible study at Westminster Chapel with these words: "I want to convert." When one speaks like that, this strongly suggests that conversion had already transpired.

Indeed, the word *convert* in the Bible is always passive in any case: one is converted. It is said of Lydia: the Lord "opened" her heart (Acts 16:14). In other words, conversion is what God does. That, then, is what lay behind Ruth's memorable statement to Naomi. It should be added that Ruth saw something in Naomi that made her want to follow her to Bethlehem.

There is much more that can be said about Ruth. For instance, we see the way she was willing to work in the fields. She was a nobody, and she knew it. She never demanded anything. Things providentially fell into place for Ruth—she met Boaz, who turned out to be a "redeemer." She married Boaz. She gave birth to Obed, who turned out to be the grandfather of King David. Boaz—and thus King David—was of the tribe of Judah, the tribe of the Messiah.

Were it not for Ruth's finest hour, when she committed her loyalty to Naomi at the cost of everything she knew and believed, the lineage of our Lord Jesus Christ would be much different (Matt. 1:5). It is remarkable how God works through his people in their moments of decision and commitment. As Paul said:

> Oh, the depth of the riches
> and the wisdom and the knowledge of God!
> How unsearchable his judgments
> and untraceable his ways! (Rom. 11:33)

I encourage you, dear reader, in the spirit of Ruth and my grandfather, to take loyalty seriously no matter what the cost may be.

TWENTY-FIVE

Joseph of Arimathea and Nicodemus, Unashamed and Unafraid

After this, Joseph of Arimathea, who was a disciple of Jesus—but secretly because of his fear of the Jews—asked Pilate that he might remove Jesus's body. Pilate gave him permission; so he came and took his body away. Nicodemus (who had previously come to him at night) also came, bringing a mixture of about seventy-five pounds of myrrh and aloes. They took Jesus's body and wrapped it in linen cloths with the fragrant spices, according to the burial custom of the Jews. There was a garden in the place where he was crucified. A new tomb was in the garden; no one had yet been placed in it. They placed Jesus there because of the Jewish day of preparation and since the tomb was nearby.

—John 19:38–42

For God has not given us a spirit of fear, but
one of power, love, and sound judgment.
—2 Timothy 1:7

Yesterday you can't alter, but your reaction to
yesterday you can. The past you cannot change,
but your response to your past you can.
—Max Lucado

When Billy Graham preached for us at Westminster Chapel, he gave his usual invitation for people to come forward, adding, "When Jesus called people to himself, he always did it publicly." At that time, I immediately thought of Nicodemus and Joseph of Arimathea. Nicodemus came to Jesus "at night" (John 3:2). Since there were no streetlights as there are in our streets today, Nicodemus probably picked an evening when there was no moon to give light. He was a "ruler" of the Jews, and a person with that stature did not want anybody to know that he was a secret admirer of Jesus. Nicodemus saw what everybody else saw and knew—that no person could perform the kind of miracles Jesus performed unless God was with him. But why did Nicodemus come to meet Jesus? The answer: the Holy Spirit.

Why do you think you are a Christian? Do you think you are better than others? Do you have a greater sense of judgment? Do you think you deserve to be a Christian? The absolute truth is: the Holy Spirit led you to invite Jesus into your heart. The Holy Spirit led you to transfer your hope from your good works to the person and work of Jesus. Dr. Martyn Lloyd-Jones often said that a Christian is one who is surprised that he or she is a Christian.

He added that if a person is not surprised to be a Christian, he wonders if he or she really is a Christian!

These things said, Jesus said that if we confess him before men, he will confess us to the Father (Matt. 10:32 KJV). The question is: What if we *don't* confess Jesus openly? I would not feel right in saying that if a person does not confess Jesus openly, he or she would not be saved. I am sure that there will be people in heaven who did not go public with their prayer to receive Christ—including people who converted on their deathbed. However, William Guthrie (1620–1665), author of *The Christian's Great Interest*, observed that we only have *one* example of a deathbed conversion in the Bible—the thief on the cross (Luke 23:42–43)—so that none would despair and that none should dare presume.

The examples of Nicodemus and the wealthy Joseph of Arimathea indicate they were secret followers of Jesus while Jesus was alive. They kept themselves in hiding for fear of the Jews. Isn't it curious that Scripture tells us this unflattering detail about them?

Fortunately, Nicodemus and Joseph's testimony didn't end with them only secretly believing in Jesus. They came out in the open and identified with Jesus right after he died—when there was nothing in it for them! That is, they were both self-effacing and had everything to lose for looking after the body of the deceased Jesus (John 19:38–42). This was an amazing moment. They wasted no time to go public when Jesus died, showing that they were unafraid and unashamed. Their finest hour was at the cross.

Paul said that "not many . . . wise from a human perspective, not many powerful, not many of noble birth" were effectually called. Indeed, most of the saved people throughout the world are ordinary, simple, and not powerful or brilliant—nobodies (1 Cor. 1:26–29). I fear that some evangelistic Christians want to focus their witness on the rich and famous, the middle class, and the intelligent! This is a mistake. The common people heard Jesus "gladly" (Mark 12:37 KJV). I believe we should preach to everyone—never ever neglecting the poor. For example, O. S. Hawkins turned the First Baptist Church of Fort Lauderdale, Florida, upside down when he announced that "we are going to reach out to those nobody wants anything to do with." He thus built one of the most amazing churches I ever saw.

Nicodemus and Joseph, however, were exceptions. Not many Pharisees were willing to identify with Jesus. Can you name any others besides Nicodemus? Nicodemus came out of hiding before Jesus was raised from the dead. Likewise, Joseph had nothing to gain in looking after the body of Jesus. William Booth (1829–1912), founder of the Salvation Army, said that if we reach the poor, the rich will join us. Jesus reached the poor—the lost, the hurting, the sinners, and the nobodies of this world. God also raised up Nicodemus and Joseph of Arimathea as examples of people with wealth and status who were willing to be identified with Jesus. Most of all, their solid faith became obvious when they overcame the fear of man and the shame of following Jesus.

TWENTY-SIX

Jacob Overcoming Joseph's Wish

When Joseph saw that [Jacob] had placed his right hand on Ephraim's head, he thought it was a mistake and took his father's hand to move it from Ephraim's head to Manasseh's. Joseph said to his father, "Not that way, my father! This one is the firstborn. Put your right hand on his head."

But his father refused and said, "I know, my son, I know! He too will become a tribe, and he too will be great; nevertheless, his younger brother will be greater than he, and his offspring will become a populous nation." So he blessed them that day, putting Ephraim before Manasseh.

—Genesis 48:17–20

Love is shown more in deeds than in words.

—St. Ignatius (d. AD 110)

Jacob, or Israel, which became his name afterward, is mentioned more than almost any other person in the Old Testament, except Moses and David. Have you ever considered Jacob and David to be the worst parents in biblical history? Me too. Nevertheless, this is still encouraging to me. My greatest sense of guilt stems from my doubts about being a decent father. If I could go back in time, I would prioritize my family. But God was gracious to me. And if God can use someone like Jacob or David, he can also use someone like me!

The first sign that Jacob was not a good parent was when he showed such ingratitude and lack of appreciation to his sons Simeon and Levi for wanting to protect and show respect for their sister, his daughter Dinah, after she had been raped by a Canaanite. Instead of thanking his sons for coming to Dinah's defense, he said to Simeon and Levi, "You have brought trouble on me, making me odious to the inhabitants of the land" (Gen. 34:30).

The second sign of Jacob being a bad parent was evident in his relationship to Joseph. Parents should not show favoritism among their children, but Jacob was guilty of doting upon Joseph. Joseph was the son of his old age and of his beloved Rachel. Jacob's favoritism revealed itself especially when he gave Joseph the renowned special coat, making the other sons jealous (37:3–4).

The third sign occurred years later, long after Joseph had been kidnapped and eventually became the prime minister (or governor) of Egypt. One of Jacob's sons had to be sent to Egypt to pacify the prime minister's suspicion that they were spies. Benjamin was Joseph's full brother, the only other son of Rachel, so Joseph requested that he be sent. After Jacob said no to this demand, he uttered these insensitive words to his sons:

> [Joseph] is dead and [Benjamin] alone is left. If anything happens to him on your journey, you will bring my gray hairs down to Sheol in sorrow. (42:38)

Imagine this! Speaking to nine of his sons (Simeon was being held back in Egypt as a ransom), Jacob actually looks directly to them and says, "He [Benjamin] alone is left." It was like these nine sons didn't exist! How do you suppose Jacob's words made these sons feel? Sadly, by this time they were undoubtedly used to being treated like this.

I have no idea whether Jacob ever felt remorse for the way he treated his ten older sons. I don't know whether he felt any guilt or responsibility for the way they had hated Joseph.

But God meant everything for good (50:20). It turned out that Joseph was alive and was even the governor—second only to the Pharaoh in Egypt! Joseph moved his father and all his relatives to Egypt, and there they had a sweet and wonderful reunion.

Some seventeen years later, knowing he was coming close to the end, Jacob wanted to bless Joseph's two sons—Manasseh (the firstborn) and Ephraim. Apparently, Jacob had been planning the details of this moment for a while. But Joseph was determined to position the two sons before Jacob conveniently so that Manasseh the firstborn easily received the greater patriarchal blessing from the right hand of the old Jacob.

Jacob and Joseph knew what was supposed to happen next. Joseph took his two boys—with Manasseh seated directly in front of Jacob's right hand. Ephraim was conveniently seated near Jacob's left hand. The right hand of the blesser was reserved in ancient Israel to bestow the greater blessing; the expectation for this blessing was that it went to the firstborn. But the old man Jacob, now one hundred and forty-seven years of age, having expressed thanks for seeing Joseph again and then embracing Joseph's two sons, stretched out his right hand toward Ephraim—the younger son—and his left hand toward Manasseh, the firstborn! Joseph thought that the aged Jacob had made a mistake and proceeded to correct his father. He placed his father's right hand on Manasseh's head, speaking: "Not that way, my father! This one is the firstborn. Put your right hand on his head."

However, Jacob refused, replying: "I know, my son, I know! He too will become a tribe, and he too will be great; nevertheless, his younger brother will be greater than he" (48:13–19).

Jacob, therefore, switched hands from the way Joseph had positioned them and refused to give Joseph's firstborn the major patriarchal blessing. This action would have disappointed his beloved Joseph. Jacob obviously did this intentionally and on purpose. But why?

Jacob finally got right what he had failed to do throughout his lifetime. Instead of following his personal love, respect, and outward affection toward his beloved Joseph, which he had done for so many years, this time Jacob listened to God. He finally showed that he loved God more than Joseph. But there is more—Jacob himself was remembering the greater blessing he himself had received from Isaac. Isaac personally preferred his firstborn, Esau. But although Jacob had stolen his father's patriarchal blessing by tricking him, Isaac stuck by his blessing (you may recall this being Isaac's finest hour). Jacob thus showed that he, like his father Isaac, chose to listen to God rather than follow his natural wishes. Jacob demonstrated by this deed that he was willing to displease his beloved Joseph and show that he loved God most after all.

In the end, Jacob put God first. He also might have sent a signal to his neglected sons through his change of heart that he was willing to displease Joseph. All's well that ends well. This was Jacob's finest hour.

TWENTY-SEVEN

Joseph and Total Forgiveness

Therefore it was not you who sent me here, but God.

—Genesis 45:8

You must totally forgive them. Until you totally forgive them, you will be in chains. Release them, and you will be released.

—Josif Ton

My wife Louise and I went through the worst moment of our lives—our darkest hour—while I served at Westminster Chapel. It is too painful to describe, and I cannot tell what happened because I learned an important lesson during this time. I confided in only one person, an old friend from Romania—Josif Ton. Honestly, I expected him to put his arm around me and say, "You ought to be angry. What they did was horrible. Get it out of your system." However, his words were surprisingly different. Josif spoke slowly and carefully in his Romanian accent:

> R. T., you must totally forgive them. Until you totally forgive them, you will be in chains. Release them, and you will be released.

This is the greatest word anybody has ever said to me.

Until recently, when I would tell this story while preaching on "Total Forgiveness," I would refer to that conversation as my finest hour. But with my new understanding of "definitive moment" and "finest hour," I feel compelled to now call that time with Josif my *definitive* moment. There was nothing self-effacing in *hearing* Josif's words. It was humbling and sobering. Carrying out Josif's word *required* being self-effacing. The challenge of Josif's word and meeting this challenge are two different things. I can tell you, reader, I face this challenge every day. I face everything I will list in this chapter every day of my life. I will let God decide whether this challenge from Josif Ton truly led to my finest hour. As Paul put it, this sort of thing will be revealed at the final judgment (1 Cor. 4:5).

As for Joseph, son of Jacob, he was a spoiled teenager. His father did him no favor in giving him the "coat of many colours" (Gen. 37:3 KJV). And yet Joseph's Heavenly Father gave him a prophetic gift. God revealed to Joseph that his eleven brothers would bow down to him one day. (v. 9). Joseph's huge mistake was telling these dreams to his brothers! They responded by plotting to kill Joseph, although after further thought they ended up kidnapping him and selling him to Ishmaelites. Joseph was separated from his father and brothers for over twenty years (vv. 18–29).

I suspect that Joseph at times imagined that God gave him these dreams so that one day he would look with vengeance on his brothers and say, "Gotcha!"—then throw the book at them. Thankfully, by the time the eleven brothers appeared in Egypt before prime minister Joseph, Joseph was a changed man. Instead of throwing the book at them, he broke down and cried unashamedly—all of Pharaoh's household heard him!

As far as I can tell, Joseph is the first example in the Bible of a person explicitly showing forgiveness. I call his act total forgiveness. He sets the pattern. We can go by his example to know whether we are truly showing total forgiveness.

If I shared with you the hurt Louise and I felt in those days, I could probably win you over. But I would also be embarrassed. This is certainly because, dear reader, *you* have endured far more pain than we did. There may be someone reading these lines who, for example, was abused as a child. Perhaps you were raped. Maybe your spouse was unfaithful. You may have suffered racial abuse. You may have endured intolerable pain from an accident or illness. But may I say this? If it could be shown that you personally have suffered more hurt, abuse, hate, embarrassment, or physical or mental anguish than anybody in your area, the angels have a word for you . . . *Congratulations!* What?! Congratulations? Yes. This is because of a principle that lies behind suffering in the will of God:

> The greater the suffering, the greater the anointing.

I have only one hope that you will be interested in this part of the book—namely, that you would like a greater anointing. Yes! I have to say, perhaps bluntly, if you are not interested in a greater anointing of the Holy Spirit, this chapter will have little relevance for you. But if you desire a greater anointing of the Spirit more than anything else in the world, this chapter is for you!

Conversely, I should add:

> The greater the anointing, the greater the suffering.

If you are blessed with a great anointing of the Holy Spirit, I can safely predict you will experience a high level of suffering. For instance, God said to Ananias concerning Saul of Tarsus:

> This man is my chosen instrument to take my name to Gentiles, kings, and Israelites. I will show him how much he must suffer for my name. (Acts 9:15–16)

God could, if he chose, grant us a great anointing without any burden of suffering. But he usually doesn't. I would lovingly urge you to accept the suffering that is almost always a part of the package of a great anointing of the Holy Spirit. I would therefore plead with you to be sure that you have totally forgiven that person or those people who have hurt you, lied to you, lied about you, betrayed you, or hurt those closest to you.

What, then, can we learn from Joseph's example of total forgiveness? I base my understanding of total forgiveness on seven proofs from Joseph.

PROOF 1: DON'T LET ANYBODY KNOW

Don't let anybody—ever—know what "they" did to you. Only God must be allowed to know. This is the way God wants it. It honors him when only he knows what these people did to you. Consider these words that came from the slaves in the cotton fields of Alabama:

> Nobody knows the troubles I've seen;
> Nobody knows but Jesus.
>
> —Anonymous

This is why Joseph commanded that everybody except his eleven brothers leave the room. He called out: "Send everyone away from me!" (Gen. 45:1). No one else was with Joseph—all the aides, attendants, servants, officials, and even the interpreter were dismissed. There was a reason—a strategy—in all that had happened before—Joseph's cup being placed in Benjamin's bag, Simeon being kept behind, the silver being placed in the brothers' bags. Joseph not only forgave his brothers but had a plan to get his entire family to move to Egypt. He wanted to make sure that no one—no one—would ever know what his brothers had done to him. Joseph knew that if the word leaked out, every Egyptian would hate his brothers. Instead, he wanted them to be loved by the Egyptians. Behind closed doors, then, Joseph revealed his identity. His dream was fulfilled perfectly without him showing the slightest bit of anger or vengeance.

There are exceptions to the principle that we never tell anyone what "they" did. Cases of rape, assault, child abuse, and comparable circumstances are different from what I am talking about. Another exception would be when you need to tell one other person for therapeutic reasons. For example, David needed a friend like Jonathan (1 Samuel 20). I told Josif Ton about my trial. I am so glad I did, because he then gave me the greatest advice of my whole life. But only tell one person—not five, not a dozen! And, yes, tell the Lord. He has big shoulders. Pour out your complaint to the Lord (Ps. 142:2)! He loves being the only one who knows.

PROOF 2: DON'T MAKE THEM LOOK BAD

So why are we so anxious to spill the beans on people who have hurt us? The answer is: we want to make them look bad. We can't bear the thought of anyone admiring these people any longer, especially if they are revered or popular! I must admit that I was severely tempted to leak the word out about what "they" did. This is a natural—but carnal—desire in nearly all who have been hurt or betrayed. Don't be surprised if the person who has hurt you is someone close to you—this makes it all the more painful.

> Living with the saints above, oh, that will be glory.
> Living with the saints below, well, that's another story.
>
> —Anonymous

That is the way God forgives you—he keeps secrets! You would not like it if God leaked what he knows about you. I would die ten thousand deaths if God were to reveal what he knows about me. *But you will never know!*

> As far as the east is from the west,
> so far has he removed
> our transgressions from us. (Ps. 103:12)

That said, when you or I point the finger at those who have hurt you—or if you reveal what they did, God says (as it were), "Whoa!" We violate a very important principle. This is why we pray in the Lord's Prayer, "Forgive us our sins, for we also forgive everyone who sins against us" (Luke 11:4 NIV).

PROOF 3: DON'T ADD GUILT TO OTHERS

You show total forgiveness when you don't add to the guilt these people may already have. Make it easy for them to forgive themselves, and *never, never, never throw* up what they have done. Joseph is a perfect example of following this advice:

> Now don't be grieved or angry with yourselves for selling me here. (Gen. 45:5)

I will admit that what often hurts the most is that these people are not sorry for what they did. It is far easier to forgive them when they are sorry. But total forgiveness includes forgiving them even when they are not sorry. May I suggest a way to get a major victory by the help of the Holy Spirit? *Forgive them when they are not sorry—or even if they don't know what they have done.* This is your chance to be like Jesus. Remember Jesus's words on the cross when praying for those who nailed in the nails: "Father, forgive them, because they do not know what they are doing" (Luke 23:34).

Truth be told, most people we have to forgive do not think they have even done anything wrong in the first place! That is what hurts. There is something in us that wants to scream to the offender, "Don't you know what you did?!"

But chances are that you have hurt people who feel this way about you. You have no idea that there is a person out there who feels wounded over something you said or did. We have all committed this fault.

Don't wait for these people to be sorry. Get your victory by forgiving them even when they do not know what they did—or even if they know and are not sorry. This is one of the best chances you will have to be like Jesus.

PROOF 4: LET THEM SAVE FACE

Moreover, *let them save face*. This ancient idea is that you enable another to preserve his or her dignity. Instead of rubbing their nose in the wrong they did, you cover for them. You act like you don't even know what they did. Indeed, this is what Joseph did with his eleven brothers. Joseph knew exactly what they did—it was wicked. But he did not uncover their wickedness.

Two things lay behind what Joseph said: (1) the twelve sons of Israel being in Egypt was predestined. God told their great-grandfather Abraham many years before that his seed would return to Canaan one day from a country not their own, namely Egypt (see Gen. 15:13); and (2) God foresaw the famine in the world as a way of attracting Israel to Egypt. This means that God was looking after the sons of Israel over twenty years before and chose Joseph out of the twelve to arrive in Egypt first to prepare for this time and "preserve life" (Gen. 45:5).

Instead of holding a grudge against the brothers and getting even, Joseph chose to overlook their evil deed and affirm God's sovereign wisdom. Joseph set the precedent of what all of us should learn: to affirm God's way of disciplining us rather than to get angry at the person or situation God chose to humble us! You will one day thank God for the person he chose in order to draw you closer to him. Don't wait—thank him now!

Total forgiveness is a choice—an act of the will. Joseph's decision became his finest hour when he chose to let his brothers save face by glorifying God's sovereign plan rather than sending them on a well-deserved guilt trip:

> Therefore it was not you who sent me here, but God. (v. 8)

I doubt a greater example of letting another save face was uttered before or since.

PROOF 5: DO NOT REVEAL THEIR SECRET

Resist the temptation to reveal others' darkest secret. What was the brothers' darkest secret? It was dipping Joseph's coat in blood to make Jacob think a wild animal had devoured his beloved Joseph. *They would rather die* than tell their father the truth of how Joseph ended up in Egypt.

Read Genesis 45:9–13 carefully. Joseph told his brothers exactly what to say to their father—he wrote the script, as it were. It was a further demonstration of letting them save face.

Chances are, you know something about someone that could destroy this person were you to reveal it. Perhaps that individual worries day and night that you will expose him or her one day. I urge you, assure this person that no one will know—ever. That is the way God is with us. That is the way Joseph was with his brothers.

PROOF 6: TOTAL FORGIVENESS IS A LIFE SENTENCE

Total forgiveness is a life sentence. By that I mean you have to forgive these people daily as long as you live. As your physician may give you a tablet that you will have to take the rest of your life—he may call it a "life sentence"—so totally forgiving another who has hurt you deeply is something you must do *every day* as long as you live. You may say, "I did it once; that is enough." Wrong. A wife may say to her husband: "I thought you forgave me." His reply: "That was yesterday." That won't do!

In Genesis 50, seventeen years later, after Jacob died, the brothers panicked. They said to themselves, "If Joseph is holding a grudge against us, he will certainly repay us for all the suffering we caused him" (v. 15). They then made up a story. They sent a message to Joseph saying that their father had commanded them before he died: "Say this to Joseph: Please forgive your brothers' transgression and their sin—the suffering they caused you" (v. 17).

Joseph immediately began to cry. The brothers then came and bowed down to him, saying: "We are your slaves!" (v. 18). But Joseph replied, "Don't be afraid" (v. 19). This displays two points: (1) that Joseph's forgiveness of his brothers seventeen years before was absolutely genuine. It was real—he truly *had* forgiven them! and (2) Joseph's forgiveness had not waned or diminished during these seventeen years; he kept it up.

PROOF 7: ASK GOD TO BLESS THEM

The last proof is connected to the previous paragraph: *you ask God to bless these people*. I cannot prove that Joseph had a prayer life in which he asked God verbally to bless his brothers every day. But listen to the words he shared with them:

> "Don't be afraid. Am I in the place of God? You planned evil against me; God planned it for good to bring about the present result—the survival of many people. Therefore don't be afraid. I will take care of you and your children." And he comforted them and spoke kindly to them. (Gen. 50:19–21)

When you can feel like this and speak like this to those who have treated you horribly and shamefully, *you're there!* This demonstrates total forgiveness. In other words, when you can ask God to bless your enemy *and mean it*, you have arrived. But I also believe that you must keep your forgiving attitude up or your heart could grow cold. The devil will also remind you of what these people did and tempt you to get upset and lose joy. I know what it is like to be awakened at 2:00 a.m. and fight a spirit of bitterness that wants to return. Yes, you pray for your enemy then in the middle of the night. You can have your finest hour during your darkest hour.

TWENTY-EIGHT

Moses and Interceding for a Nation

So he said he would have destroyed them—
if Moses his chosen one
had not stood before him in the breach
to turn his wrath away from destroying them.

—Psalm 106:23

God has no greater controversy with his people than this, that with boundless promises to believing prayer, there are so few who actually give themselves unto intercession.

—A. T. Pierson (1837–1911)

Moses was probably the greatest human being in world history—next to Jesus. If the Old Testament was summed up in one word, it would be Moses. The New Testament summed up in one word would be Jesus. "For the law was given through Moses; grace and truth came through Jesus Christ" (John 1:17).

The life of Moses is marked by defining moments. But what was his finest hour? Let us start by looking at his early life.

Moses's first defining moment was set by his mother, who did not resign herself to seeing her newborn son destroyed, but rather placed him in a basket and watched him drift away on the Nile River. Pharaoh's daughter found baby Moses in the bulrushes and raised him as an Egyptian, making him a grandson of the Pharaoh. But Moses would have been circumcised before his parents kissed him goodbye—hence, he grew up knowing that he was different from other Egyptian boys. He therefore began to realize that those Hebrew slaves, toiling under his grandfather Pharaoh, were actually his people.

The day came when Moses could put it off no longer; he wanted to endear himself to these slaves. Whether he knew he would be sent by God one day to come to their rescue, I don't know. He had no apparent specific command from God at that stage that we know of, and yet I cannot help but think that he had a God-given instinct to somehow identify with these Hebrews. In any case, Moses jumped the gun: he killed an Egyptian and was discovered. He then knew he could not return to the palace but had to make it on his own. Life would never be the same again for Moses. We learn from Hebrews 11:24–25 that behind all this was his refusal to be the son of Pharaoh's daughter and his decision to suffer with the Hebrews.

God did not begin to use Moses until he was eighty—this shows that God is patient! Moses began to discover the true God for himself, but in stages. At the burning bush he began to learn more about God, who identified himself as the God of Abraham, Isaac, and Jacob. Moses also found out that we are not allowed to figure out some things about God, but can only respond by worshiping him (Ex. 3:6). This is when he received divine orders to return to Egypt to deliver the Israelites from Pharaoh. This was a momentous occasion. God identified himself to Moses as "I AM WHO I AM" (v. 14). Moses consequently felt inadequate and God showed him that his staff would be essential to his power and leadership, turning it into a snake (4:1–3). Feeling even more inadequate, Moses suggested that God send someone else, and the Lord did agree that Aaron should accompany him (vv. 13–17). But God gave advance notice that the days ahead would be hard. And, strange as it may seem, God said he would "harden" Pharaoh's heart (v. 21) so that he would refuse to let the Israelites go. The people, on the other hand, were thrilled to hear that God had sent Moses and Aaron to deliver them from Pharaoh (v. 31). This pivotal encounter of Moses with God is an example of how you and I must bow to the mystery of God's sovereignty and not try to figure everything out.

Perhaps a case could be made that Moses's finest hour was in his initial confrontation with Pharaoh and in subsequent challenges to the king of Egypt. His first bold stand before Pharaoh was when he said:

> This is what the LORD, the God of Israel, says: "Let my people go, so that they may hold a festival for me in the wilderness." (5:1)

I always smile when I read Pharaoh's response to Moses: "I don't know the LORD," possibly the greatest understatement in all Holy Writ! In any case, that was the beginning: "I will not let Israel go" (v. 2). But the worst now followed. Not only would Pharaoh not let the Israelites go; he rebuked and insulted Moses by ordering that the slaves in Egypt would no longer be supplied with straw for bricks, but would have to produce the same quota of bricks by getting their own straw. This was a backfire for which Moses or Aaron or the people of Israel were not prepared. The Israelites complained to Moses, accusing him of making things worse, and Moses complained to God, *implicitly* accusing him of making things worse (vv. 21–22). But the Lord, rather than rebuking Moses, sympathetically replied, "Now you will see what I will do to Pharaoh" (6:1). This shows how a gracious God understands what we are feeling. Moses's complaint to God was done with reverence and respect; we all need to learn from that example.

And yet Moses would learn still more about God during his bold confrontations with Pharaoh. For example, Moses discovered that the name LORD—Yahweh—was not known by his forefathers Abraham, Isaac, and Jacob but was now revealed to him (6:3)! This is a demonstration that while we serve the Lord, we continue to learn about the infinite God—even great leaders continue to learn. We will learn more and more and more about God here on earth and more and more and more about God in heaven.

Recall the plagues on Egypt. Pharaoh continued to refuse Moses's warning, so God continued to send one plague after another: (1) the water turning to blood, (2) the frogs, (3) gnats, (4) flies, (5) death of livestock, (6) boils, (7) hail, (8) locusts, (9) darkness, and (10) death of the firstborn (Ex. 7–11). These plagues show how God is in total control of nature. They show his awareness of what brings pain. They show how God grasps everything that happens in minute detail. God might have secured the ultimate response from Pharaoh with the first plague.

But through Pharaoh's delay, God, as we would learn, would receive more glory. *All that God does or allows is for his glory.* Now, dear reader, note: how you react to this truth about God is a good sign of what you think about the God of the Bible. According to Jonathan Edwards, the one thing that Satan cannot produce in human beings is a love for the glory of God. All people are born with a propensity to hate God; Edwards called all people God's natural enemies. These things said, if you, reader, love the God of glory, this is a true and valid sign that you are born again. But as Moses learned more and more about God, so you and I also learn about the God of glory in stages. We may begin our pilgrimage of knowing God in shock and disappointment. So did Moses! But he found God to be true, faithful, reliable, wonderful, gracious, good, and upright at the end of the day. So will you.

Could the tenth plague be Moses's finest hour? This plague finally broke Pharaoh; it was also the occasion for the Passover. This was an unprecedented moment displaying the importance, relevance, and power of the shedding of blood. Moses instructed the Israelites to do what had never been done: they were to butcher a lamb and eat it, but keep its blood for a moment that would be forever and ever called Passover. Moses announced,

> This is what the Lord says: About midnight I will go throughout Egypt, and every firstborn male in the land of Egypt will die, from the firstborn of Pharaoh who sits on his throne to the firstborn of the servant girl who is at the grindstones, as well as every firstborn of the livestock . . . so that you may know that the Lord makes a distinction between Egypt and Israel. (11:4–5, 7)

God further instructed the people of Israel through Moses: "Take some of the blood and put it on the two doorposts and the lintel of the houses where they eat [the Passover meal]" (12:7). God added:

> I will pass through the land of Egypt on that night and strike every firstborn male in the land of Egypt, both people and animals. I am the LORD; I will execute judgments against all the gods of Egypt. The blood on the houses where you are staying will be a distinguishing mark for you; when I see the blood, I will pass over you. (vv. 12–13)

This plague worked. At midnight the Lord struck every firstborn male in the land of Egypt. Pharaoh summoned Moses and Aaron during the night and said,

> Get out . . . go, worship the LORD . . . and also bless me. (vv. 31–32)

However, although the people of Egypt were thrilled to see the back of the Israelites, Pharaoh began to regret his decision. Shortly after Moses and the children of Israel left, Pharaoh ordered his army to pursue them. At the bottom of this episode—again, this being one of God's mysterious ways—the Lord "hardened the heart of Pharaoh king of Egypt" (14:8). Why? "Then I will receive glory by means of Pharaoh and all his army, and the Egyptians will know that I am the LORD" (v. 4). And yet one of the ways of the Lord is—always—that what God wills is also what is best for you and me. Always. Every time. I urge you, as much as possible, to learn to never complain about God's dealings in your life. I admit that it is not always easy to do this in the moment. This is why James said we should count it "pure joy" when we fall into all sorts of trials (James 1:2 NIV). Why? Because we will be glad eventually. James, therefore, says, as it were, "Do it now"!

But when the Israelites saw the Egyptians coming after them, they were "terrified" and cried out to the Lord for help. The Israelites sadly blamed Moses: "Is it because there are no graves in Egypt that you have taken us away to die in the wilderness? . . . It would have been better for us to serve the Egyptians than to die in the wilderness." (Ex. 14:10–12).

But Moses did not panic; he sought to encourage the despondent Israelites. Could this, therefore, have been Moses's finest hour? He began by responding:

> Don't be afraid. Stand firm and see the LORD's salvation that he will accomplish for you today; for the Egyptians you see today, you will never see again. The LORD will fight for you, and you must be quiet. (vv. 13–14)

However, Moses may have been afraid too! It seems like a verse might have been left out, which could have said, "Moses cried to the Lord." I mention this because the next verse actually says:

> The LORD said to Moses, "Why are you crying out to me? . . . Lift up your staff, stretch out your hand over the sea, and divide it so that the Israelites can go through the sea on dry ground." (vv. 15–16)

God added that he was going to harden the hearts of the Egyptians to pursue the Israelites one more time so that he would get more glory (v. 17).

Moses stretched out his hand over the sea. "The LORD drove the sea back with a powerful east wind and turned the sea into dry land" (v. 21). The Israelites then went through the sea on dry ground. When the Egyptians followed them, Moses stretched out his hand over the sea and the water rushed back, covering the chariots and horsemen plus the entire army of Pharaoh. "Not even one of them survived" (v. 28). Consequently, "The people feared the LORD and believed in him and in his servant Moses" (v. 31).

Was this Moses's finest hour? Was the night of Passover Moses's finest hour? All he did was in utter obedience to God, who certainly got all the glory. The Passover and the crossing of the Red Sea were undoubtedly Moses's most exciting, memorable, and thrilling moments. But I am inclined to believe that his finest and greatest moment, if being self-effacing is the key criterion, came later.

I will pass by some memorable moments during the forty years that followed the exodus—the manna and quail that was provided (Exodus 16), the water that came from the rock (Exodus 17:1–7), the giving of the Ten Commandments (Exodus 20), and details of the civil and ceremonial laws (Exodus 21–31).

But one day God appeared to be completely "fed up," if I may put it that way. His anger broke out against Israel when it worshiped the golden calf. It was the most flagrant idolatry Moses had witnessed, and even Aaron was complicit in this wicked act. Moses was grieved and heartbroken for Israel. God said to him:

> [The Israelites] have quickly turned from the way I commanded them; they have made for themselves an image of a calf. They have bowed down to it, sacrificed to it, and said, "Israel, these are your gods, who brought you up from the land of Egypt" . . . I have seen this people, and they are indeed a stiff-necked people. Now leave me alone, so that my anger can burn against them and I can destroy them. Then I will make you into a great nation. (32:8–10)

The account in Deuteronomy also reiterates God's words:

> Leave me alone, and I will destroy them and blot out their name under heaven. Then I will make you into a nation stronger and more numerous than they. (9:14)

Here was Moses's chance—his big chance—to get the fallen Israelites off his back. Aaron would also get the punishment he deserved. God even said to Moses, "Leave me alone"!

However, Moses responded, in my words: "No! You cannot do this. Your great name is at stake. What will they say back in Egypt? They will laugh at the Lord and say that he was not able to bring them into the land of Canaan." Then Moses fell down in the presence of the Lord upon Mount Sinai. He prayed forty days and forty nights, saying:

> Lord God, do not annihilate your people, your inheritance, whom you redeemed through your greatness and brought out of Egypt with a strong hand. Remember your servants Abraham, Isaac, and Jacob. Disregard this people's stubbornness, and their wickedness and sin. Otherwise, those in the

> land you brought us from will say, "Because the LORD wasn't able to bring them into the land he had promised them, and because he hated them, he brought them out to kill them in the wilderness. But they are your people, your inheritance, whom you brought out by your great power and outstretched arm." (vv. 26–29)

God heard Moses's intercession for Israel and a nation was preserved.

This was Moses's finest hour.

Let me tell you why this appeal of Moses means so much to me. I have been the pastor of six churches in my lifetime—in Palmer, Tennessee (1955–56), Carlisle, Ohio (1962–63), Fort Lauderdale, Florida (1968–70), Salem, Indiana (1971–73), Lower Heyford, Oxfordshire, England (1974–76), and London (1977–2002). In most of these I have had some measure of opposition. In Carlisle I publicly preached that Jesus was God, and some of my members complained to the local ministerial association of the denomination, which brought ecclesiastical charges against me. I pled guilty. The church in Carlisle voted fourteen to thirteen to let me remain as pastor, but I resigned shortly afterward. I have never had any other opposition like that. Those were rough and horrible days for Louise and me. I left Ohio with a mental block from which I have never recovered.

I am sharing the details of this trial because I hate to think of what I would have said back to God had he come to me in 1963 with a proposition similar to the one he offered Moses during the incident of the golden calf. I fear I would *not* have interceded on behalf of my enemies. I am afraid I would have said, "Wonderful, Lord! Thank you, thank you! Go for them."

I *like to think* I might have interceded on that congregation's behalf in more recent years, especially after Josif Ton came into my life. But I doubt I would have done so in 1963. I was hurt and very bitter. In fact, I had to take a break from the pastorate, selling vacuum cleaners door-to-door in Fort Lauderdale from 1964 to 1968.

This facet in Moses's life puts me to shame as I look back on my years of ministry before I met Josif Ton. Moses's bold intercession also reveals how well he knew the Lord! How dare Moses talk to God Almighty like that! *But he did.* And Moses got away with it because he knew that God was gracious. As Jonah said, "I knew that you are a gracious and compassionate God" (Jonah 4:2).

The truth is, God wanted Moses to respond exactly the way he did!

God speaks to us at our level. The eternal God, who declares "the end from the beginning" (Isa. 46:10) and who is the "First and the Last," wants you and me to know him intimately. God lamented that the children of Israel did not know his "ways" (Heb. 3:10). *But Moses knew God's ways!* God was delighted with Moses's intercession and initially challenged Moses to demonstrate not only his wrath but also his mercy. This is why the psalmist praised Moses for his standing in the gap:

> So he said he would have destroyed them—
> if Moses his chosen one
> had not stood before him in the breach
> to turn his wrath away from destroying them.
> (Ps. 106:23)

We learn more about faithful leading in Moses's intercession than from all his victories in a long life of following God and leading his people out of Egypt. God wants more people to intercede; I remember reading a tract a long time ago entitled "Where are the Intercessors?" It is truly unselfish praying when you intercede with God on behalf of someone. Would you regard yourself as an intercessor?

TWENTY-NINE

Stephen and Finishing Well

Lord, do not hold this sin against them!
—Acts 7:60

Forgiveness is an act of the will, and the will can function regardless of the temperature of the heart.
—Corrie ten Boom (1892–1983)

Stephen has been my favorite biblical character for as long as I can remember. The words from Acts 6:10, "And they were not able to resist the wisdom and the spirit by which [Stephen] spake" (KJV) have gripped me as much as any other verse in the Bible. Because I think of the apostles as extraordinarily gifted (rightly or wrongly), I have minimized the importance of diaconal ministry, even regarding Stephen as a layperson. But when I consider his knowledge of the Old Testament, shown in his defense to the Sanhedrin in Acts 7, I ask whether many full-time ministers today have his anointing!

We can thank the church's first squabble that we know anything about Stephen. (I might wish all church quarrels ended up as beneficially as this one!) The problem was a rivalry between Hebrew Jews and Hellenistic (Greek) Jews. The Hebrew Jews championed themselves as a cut above the Greek Jews in culture and social standing. As the English people regard their English language superior to American English language and the Spanish people consider their Spanish language and culture a cut above Cuban or Mexican Spanish language and culture, so this same sort of issue existed two thousand years ago in the church. The Greek Jews felt that their widows were being neglected in financial support. The twelve apostles were forced to get involved in this issue and therefore did not have time to teach and preach the Gospel—which was their priority. So the apostles got all the believers together. They pointed out this problem and proposed, "Select from among you seven men of good reputation, full of the Spirit and wisdom, whom we can appoint to this duty. But we will devote ourselves to prayer and to the ministry of the word" (6:3–4).

This plan seemed good to the whole church, and the first on the list of seven men is Stephen: "a man full of faith and the Holy Spirit" (v. 5). The consequence of this decision was that the "word of God spread, the disciples in Jerusalem increased greatly in number, and a large group of priests became obedient to the faith" (v. 7). Luke also mentions that Stephen, "full of grace and power, was performing great wonders and signs among the people" (v. 8). But opposition arose and some people began to argue with Stephen. However, "They were unable to stand up against his wisdom and the Spirit by whom he was speaking" (v. 10).

Several things strike me about Stephen. Consider his wisdom. Some might think that being filled with the Spirit automatically gives you wisdom. Apparently not—wisdom is not listed as a fruit of the Spirit in Galatians 5:23–24. Furthermore, Luke says that Stephen was filled with the Spirit *and wisdom*. He obviously had the gift of wisdom, as in 1 Corinthians 12:8. Wisdom is the way we *use* knowledge. I've known precious saints of God who had the fruit of the Spirit but seemed to have no wisdom! Yet Stephen had both. Wisdom is getting God's opinion; it is the presence of the *mind* of the Spirit. The Holy Spirit knows the right thing to say at the right time. Wisdom is like having 20/20 foresight vision (we all have 20/20 hindsight vision). According to James, we all can have wisdom—just ask God (James 1:5); it begins with the fear of God, according to Solomon (Prov. 9:10). Wisdom is not your IQ; it is God unveiling his own opinion regarding what to do. Stephen had so much wisdom that his opponents could not dismiss him.

Stephen's wisdom gave him his boldness and fearlessness. Having shown his vast knowledge of the Old Testament, he was unafraid to *apply* what he had taught. Sounding a bit like John the Baptist, Stephen denounced the members of the Sanhedrin: "You stiff-necked people with uncircumcised hearts and ears! You are always resisting the Holy Spirit. As your ancestors did, you do also" (Acts 7:51).

I would call Stephen the perfect example of a person who had an equal measure of the Word and Spirit. Stephen not only performed wonders and signs among the people (6:8), but his address to the Sanhedrin began with his biblical understanding of God as a "God of glory" (7:2).

Oh, how I would like to have as much of God as Stephen had! Simultaneous with the anger of the members of the Sanhedrin (who were so furious that they "gnashed their teeth at him"), Stephen saw the "glory of God and Jesus standing at the right hand of God." He thought everybody present was also beholding it, and said, "Look, I see the heavens opened and the Son of Man standing at the right hand of God!" Instead of opening their hearts to the Lord, the members of the Sanhedrin "yelled at the top of their voices, covered their ears, and together rushed against him. They dragged him out of the city and began to stone him" (7:54–58).

I pause. I ask, what was the secret to Stephen's extraordinary anointing of the Spirit and his close relationship to the Lord Jesus Christ? These undoubtedly can be traced partly to Stephen's vast knowledge of Holy Scripture. I am sure he was also a man of prayer. But do all who have a prayer life and solid Bible knowledge have such an anointing? Probably not. I think that Stephen's secret is to be found in his very last words just before he died. As he was being stoned, Stephen knelt and prayed: "Lord, do not hold this sin against them!" (v. 60). Was this amazing demonstration of total forgiveness the sudden result of a fresh filling of the Spirit as he was dying? I don't think so; total forgiveness is an act of the will. Rather, Stephen's forgiveness of his enemies was the fruit of a lifestyle existing before this historic moment. This was Stephen's finest hour.

Please ponder Stephen's dying prayer for a moment. It is one thing to ask God to *forgive* our enemy. That is a good but hard decision to make. Such a request goes against human nature since we instinctively want to get vengeance. And yet it is another thing to ask God to *bless* our enemy. That is extremely hard to do. I would have thought that blessing our enemy may be the highest level of showing total forgiveness. But look carefully at Stephen's prayer—it is a step beyond any prayer I have come across. Other than Jesus's praying for the soldiers and priests while on the cross (Luke 23:34), Stephen's dying prayer is the most challenging and most convicting prayer ever prayed that I know of. To pray that God will not hold this sin against these wicked men means praying that God will not later remember their sin at all—either to expose them or punish them. Ever.

Stephen was at his most vulnerable moment and on the verge of death. He didn't have to forgive or pray for those desiring his death. Technically, this moment was not self-effacing. But Stephen had nothing to gain from an earthly point of view—and yet he prayed for his enemies. That is why this was his finest hour.

When I think of particular people who have hurt me over the years, would I ask God not to hold their sin against them at the *judgment seat of Christ*? I am, I think, truly willing to wait for everything to be revealed at that judgment seat. This is because the whole truth will come out regarding what they have said and done; I have greatly looked forward to this open display. To be totally honest, that great exposé is what has kept me going and helped me to be quiet! Paul says that everybody—everybody!—will see the truth at the judgment of what people have said about us and done to us, whether to bless or discredit or hurt us:

> So don't judge anything prematurely, before the Lord comes, who will both bring to light what is hidden in darkness and reveal the intentions of the hearts. (1 Cor. 4:5)

First Corinthians 4:5 refers to the second coming and the judgment seat of Christ. Everything will be out in the open at that point. Then—not before. Only then. I have taught and preached that this moment will be worth waiting for. I have actually said that I want to see the look on my enemies' faces when everything is revealed.

But Stephen's prayer shames me.

Having looked carefully at Stephen's prayer, I see that it is a higher level of grace than merely forgiving or blessing one's enemy. It is praying that what they said and did will *never be known*. You might say that God will not answer Stephen's prayer since God declared that vengeance belongs to himself (Deut. 32:35; Rom. 12:19). After all, as seen earlier, Paul himself looked forward to when the total truth of what people had done to him would be revealed; everything would be out in the open. So, was Stephen's prayer merely a showpiece of godliness? Or did he mean what he prayed? I reply: Stephen was not playing games. He saw the Lord Jesus standing to welcome him home. Thus, Stephen absolutely meant what he said in that prayer.

Stephen was not bargaining for more anointing in his dying moments. He could not have thought to pray like this if he had not previously made a decision regarding forgiving his enemies. In fact, he had made this decision *before* he was chosen to be a deacon! As I said earlier, forgiveness is an act of the will. Forgiveness is what lay behind Stephen's wisdom when he disputed with Jews who made up lies about what he said (Acts 6:12–14). It was the secret to his anointing when he boldly and articulately addressed the Sanhedrin (7:1–50). It is what caused his face to shine like an angel (6:15). The secret to Stephen's anointing was that he had *already* possessed such depths of forgiveness—totally, utterly, and absolutely overlooking his enemies' evil words and deeds. Such a forgiving spirit preceded Stephen's anointing. Frankly, I have not had a spirit like this. But I want it now!

THIRTY

The Nameless Widow and Her Finest Hour

[Jesus] looked up and saw the rich dropping their offerings into the temple treasury. He also saw a poor widow dropping in two tiny coins. "Truly I tell you," he said, "this poor widow has put in more than all of them. For all these people have put in gifts out of their surplus, but she out of her poverty has put in all she had to live on."

—Luke 21:1–4

But many who are first will be last, and the last first.

—Matthew 19:30

God is watching us, but he loves us so much that He can't take His eyes off us. We may lose sight of God, but He never loses sight of us.

—Greg Laurie

The final judgment—the scariest time in the history of the world—will reveal some amazing things. It is the ultimate Day of days. All history has been moving toward this Omega Point. It is when God will clear his name. He will vindicate his Son, as well as his word and his integrity. The ancient prophets warned that this day would come (Amos 5:18–24; Isaiah 66; Joel 3). It will be a day to show the truth about everything—especially about God and the reason for evil—and righteousness and truth will be transparently vindicated. The truth about that unfair trial will emerge. The person who got away with murder will be exposed. Adolf Hitler and Joseph Stalin will stand before the Supreme Judge. The blind, the deaf, the crippled, the mentally handicapped, the person who grew up without a father, the abused wife, the wife beater, the crooked politician, and the one with no opportunity for a good education will—at last—get noticed and be given due recognition. Those who never heard the gospel will stand before a just God. The final judgment will reveal who is saved and who is lost. It will also show who among the saved receives a reward and who is saved by fire. Everything will be out in the open.

The final judgment has been a truth which the people of God have long held to. When Jesus referred to "that day" (Matt. 7:22), everyone knew what he meant: a day is coming when God will judge the world. Paul said that God has "set a day when he is going to judge the world in righteousness by the man he has appointed" (Acts 17:31). Jesus Christ will judge the "living and the dead" when he comes a second time (2 Tim. 4:1). "It is appointed for people to die once—and after this, judgment" (Heb. 9:27). Finally, Jesus said:

> For nothing is concealed that won't be revealed, and nothing hidden that won't be made known and brought to light. (Luke 8:17)

> I tell you that on the day of judgment people will have to account for every careless word they speak. (Matt. 12:36)

As we have seen in this book, Paul looked forward to the judgment when God will "both bring to light what is hidden in darkness and reveal the intentions of the hearts" (1 Cor. 4:5).

When Jesus said that many who are first will be last and the last first, he referred largely to the final judgment. For example, many who have a high profile now will be humiliated then. Many who are famous now will be barely respected then. Many who are the head now will be the tail then.

I also think of that poor widow who put two small coins into the temple treasury. She had no idea who was watching. She did not know that her Creator was watching, that the most important person in history was watching, and that the man who would save the world by his death was watching. But his disciples were apparently not watching. Jesus *summoned* them and commented about the poor widow (Mark 12:43). He *called* his disciples to him to share his observation (NIV).

This widow had no idea that in God's eyes she was the biggest and most generous giver in Jerusalem.

Jesus missed nothing. A woman who was disabled by an evil spirit for over eighteen years so that she was bent over and could not straighten up was noticed by Jesus. He called out to her and healed her (Luke 13:11–13). Another time Jesus noticed a widow mourning her dead son in a funeral procession. He walked over to the grieving widow and said, "Don't cry," and then raised the man back to life (7:13 NIV).

Again, Jesus missed nothing. To this day he misses nothing. He saw the rich putting in their offerings. It is likely that the rabbis and temple officials were most appreciative of the "deep pocket" givers that supported the temple financially. They may not even have known that there was a widow—a poor one—who put in two small coins. Nor would they have likely known—as Jesus did—that she gave not only out of her poverty but put in "all she had to live on" (21:4). Only Jesus knew that.

We don't even know the widow's name. Jesus recognized what probably no one else had recognized. There are nameless people who serve God that don't get noticed. They have no profile at all. They are not appreciated nor recognized. A widow is almost certainly one of the loneliest human beings on the planet. This is why James said that pure religion is to look after "orphans and widows in their distress" (James 1:27).

When Billy Graham preached for us at Westminster Chapel, he spoke on "loneliness." No one who was present will ever forget that sermon. I am ashamed to say that it had not crossed my mind to deal with a subject like that before. Billy reflected the heart of Jesus that night.

Jesus watched that widow having her finest hour. She is an example of how nameless people may have their finest hour. They are never known on earth—but they will be heroes in heaven.

Would you call yourself a person of low profile? Be encouraged. If you get praised by the only true God, you have accomplished the greatest victory that is possible on this planet. God's praise comes to those who are not trying to impress people but want his praise alone. Anyone may apply for this—the rich, the poor, the married, the divorced, the single person, the widow, the widower, the famous, the unknown, the politician, the janitor, the lorry driver, the secretary, the physician, or the lawyer. If you are used to getting recognition, get ready to be treated like everyone else. If you are not known generally, get ready to hear from the Lord Jesus Christ himself, "Well done."

Jesus is watching you now. His followers may not notice you. You may feel forgotten, neglected, or rejected. But Jesus is watching. Turn to him, and your finest hour will be coming soon.

CONCLUSION

Do All Who Have a Finest Hour Get Rewarded for It?

For whoever wants to save his life will lose it, but whoever loses his life because of me will find it.

—Matthew 16:25

It is impossible to be faithful to Jesus Christ and not incur the opposition of the world.

—William Still (1911–1997)

When I set out to write this book, my mind was on other writing projects. As I mentioned in the introduction, seemingly inspired thoughts occurred to me about the notable biblical characters David and Elisha. What more could be said about the lives of David and Elisha that hasn't already been said or written? But my thoughts felt fresh and focused especially on moments in the lives of biblical heroes when they didn't appear heroic. Would the important people in the Bible still be important or worth learning about without their most self-effacing moments? I suspect not. And, hence, these self-effacing moments that I call their "finest hours" inspired me to write this book. These moments required no special anointing. And since self-effacing moments might happen to anyone, ordinary believers like you and me can learn from them about God and his rewards for faithfulness.

It should by now be apparent that we cannot make our finest hour happen. We may not even know when our finest hour is at hand, but if we have lived to honor and please God we will surely experience our finest hour.

I want to encourage you to follow Jesus daily with a view to being self-effacing and living for his glory. There is no doubt in my mind that God will eventually bring a situation to test you and me, although we may not know it is a test at that time. For instance, I am sure that Joseph's brothers were unaware that they were being tested when in the providence of God they found themselves in a position where they had to make a decision about Joseph's cup in Benjamin's bag. They were tested to see whether they were changed men. The brothers could have left Benjamin to suffer severe punishment by allowing the prime minister of Egypt to incarcerate him for the crime of theft. This test would show whether they would abandon their half-brother Benjamin as they did Joseph. But the ten brothers had indeed changed and demonstrated utter loyalty and care for Benjamin. That was their finest hour (Gen. 44).

I believe every Christian can have his or her finest hour. We may ask whether a finest hour is its own reward? Or does having a finest hour mean that there still is more—that you will be rewarded further for having a finest hour? I say "yes" to both questions. One's finest hour is certainly its own reward. And, yes, one will also be rewarded for a finest hour—in some way. You may receive the awareness that you have pleased God. Knowing that you please God, as Enoch did (Heb. 11:5), is an incalculable blessing. I encourage you once more to turn to my recent book *Pleasing God* to understand this better.

The Bible consistently appeals to our self-interest to get our obedience. There are no exceptions here. Abraham was enticed to leave his country because God would make his name great (Gen. 12:1–3). Moses left Pharaoh's palace because he knew God would reward him (Heb. 11:26). Malachi promised that giving God a tithe of our increase would guarantee us a blessing (Mal. 3:10). Jesus also said:

> Do not judge, and you will not be judged. Do not condemn, and you will not be condemned. Forgive, and you will be forgiven. Give, and it will be given to you; a good measure—pressed down, shaken together, and running over—will be poured into your lap. For with the measure you use, it will be measured back to you. (Luke 6:37–38)

I read Luke 6:37–38 every single day for almost ten years when we were in London. I hoped to be rewarded for honoring the promises of those verses. Was I? Yes. I also hoped revival at Westminster Chapel would be part of the reward. Did it happen? No.

I know many Christians resist the idea of a reward or of being rewarded at the judgment seat of Christ. I hope I'm not being unfair, but I wonder if those sincere Christians who disdain the notion of a reward really know their Bibles! They think it is more admirable or more honoring to God to labor without being rewarded for it. Are they being just a bit self-righteous?

But God, in fact, loves to reward obedience. He promises to reward obedience. Obedience means utter faithfulness to Jesus Christ. A reward will follow that, yes!

Caution: opposition also follows your obedience. The devil does not like your faithfulness, and he will raise up enemies. They may come from the world. They may come from the church. They may come from your best friends—or even your family. God will test your obedience. This is when total forgiveness on our part *must* enter our minds and hearts—or kick in, if I may use that expression.

No one said obedience would be easy. But are you going to be rewarded? Yes! God himself, however, will be the one to determine *how* that reward is meted out to you. In my own case, my reward was having more insight into the Bible. It was what I actually wanted. I wanted revival, too, but God seemed to say, "Enough." Insight, yes. Revival, no—at least so far! I'm still alive and hope to see the greatest awakening in history while I yet live.

So, does it follow that we get what we want for obeying the Lord? No. This is where we need to think soberly and carefully. Not all are rewarded equally. For example, Jesus told Peter how he would die but also told him to shut up when Peter wanted to know what would happen to John (John 21:18–22). God also has said that he will have compassion on whom he will have compassion and be gracious to whom he would be gracious (Ex. 33:19; Rom. 9:15). That is the privilege and prerogative for being God. Some resent this. I hope you don't resent it, but rather love it. God may elevate your status in the church—or even in the world. He could make you the head or eye of the body and thus give you a high profile in your church. Or he could make you the stomach or pancreas of the body and give you the gift of helping others (1 Cor. 12:12–31). He could make you president. Or prime minister. Or help you to win a Nobel Prize. On the other hand, God could exalt your enemy and make you feel that he has deserted you. But trust him and love him whichever way he chooses to use you. By the way, feeling deserted is almost certainly a temporary feeling. God will not always accuse us or appear angry (Ps. 103:9). He will show up—never too late and never too early, but always just on time!

A word of caution about rewards: I am not talking about the "prosperity gospel" notion that all Christians should have wealth or be healed. Or that we can name it and claim it—speak or pray what we want into our possession. That is not biblical at all! However, Jesus did promise to supply our *need* when we seek the kingdom of God "first" (Matt. 6:31–33). That is what is promised. The need essentially means food, shelter, and clothing. It is true that God makes some people rich, while others live day by day with just enough to live on. Why? God is sovereign. But seeking first his kingdom means that we must seek primarily to know God himself. We must put him absolutely first. We must want *him*. After all, Paul's ardent desire was *to know Christ* (Phil. 3:10). He consequently learned to live with or without a lot of comfort (4:12). David also showed that he was indeed a man after God's own heart when he made a clear choice to have *God's approval and the presence of God himself* rather than the return of the kingship. And God did restore his kingdom to him.

So, God blesses all who obey him, but he does not bless all in the same measure.

You may not be Moses. Or Abraham. Or Samuel. Or Deborah. Or Sarah. But the willingness to be self-effacing and resigned utterly to the glory and sovereignty of God is the best way to live.

The reward—whatever God chooses for you and me—is worth it. Furthermore, fully accepting what God sends—whether or not it is what you want—can be your finest hour.

I pray that God gives you a finest hour and rewards you richly for living a self-effacing life that seeks the glory of God alone. You will not be disappointed!

May the grace of our Lord Jesus Christ, the love of God the Father, and the fellowship of the Holy Spirit by the sprinkling of the blood of Jesus be with you now and ever more. Amen.

Afterword

We have come once again to the end of one of R. T. Kendall's God-anointed, eye-opening, and thought-provoking volumes. As we journeyed through these pages, we were inspired by the "finest hours" of David and Daniel, Rebekah and Rahab, Jacob and Joseph, Elijah and Elisha, Moses and Mordecai, and many others who, in the midst of all the valleys of life, reached a mountain top that became their very own "finest hour."

One very important question remains as we prepare to close this book: What about you? . . . What was your finest hour? While there is a difference in a defining moment in life and a finest hour in life, there is a point at which they intersect. It is possible that before you turn the final page of this book, you may experience a divine encounter when your own finest hour results in a truly defining moment in life.

Perhaps along the way God's Spirit has been nudging you to what could become your own finest hour: that point in time when you intersect with the defining moment of placing your total trust in Jesus Christ alone for your salvation. After all, heaven is God's personal gift to you. It can never be earned nor deserved. We, like everyone in this volume, are all sinners, have fallen short of God's perfect standard, and cannot save ourselves. God is a God of love, but the Bible is clear that He is also a God of justice and must punish sin. This is where Jesus steps into what can become your finest hour. He is the holy and sinless God-man who came to take your own sins upon Himself and die on the cross in your place, bearing God's punishment which you deserved for your sin. Then, on the third day after His death, He arose and is alive today. But just knowing these facts will not result in a defining moment in your life, much less a finest hour. Rather, you must transfer your own trust from all your human efforts to Christ alone, placing your faith in Him.

If this is the desire of your heart at this very moment, the Bible promises: "Everyone who calls on the name of the Lord will be saved" (Romans 10:13). Believe it . . . and you can join Simon Peter in his own prayer on the Sea of Galilee. Just say it: "Lord, save me!" (Matt. 14:30). The following is a suggested prayer you can pray in your own heart . . . right now . . . wherever you are reading these words:

Dear Lord Jesus, I know that I have sinned. I know that in and of myself I do not deserve eternal life with You. Please forgive me for my sin. Thank You for taking my own sin in Your own body and dying in my place. I believe Your promise that by calling on You in repentance and faith I can be saved. Lord, save me . . . come into my life. I accept Your free and gracious offer of eternal life. In Jesus's name, Amen.

Now, as an expression of the fact that you believe God is not a liar and keeps His promises, just whisper this prayer: "Lord, thank You for coming into my life this very moment to become my very own personal Lord and Savior." A simple prayer cannot save you . . . but Jesus can . . . and will! Take Him at His word and claim his promise: "Truly I tell you, anyone who believes has eternal life" (John 6:47).

Welcome to God's forever family. Mark this moment . . . it is a defining moment in your life. And, without question, it is also your very own finest hour.

O. S. Hawkins

Prophetic Integrity: Aligning Our Words with God's Word

R. T. Kendall (Foreword by Dr. Michael L. Brown)

What happens when prophets are wrong?

In 2020, many Christians claiming to be prophets said God had told them that Donald Trump would be reelected as president. Over thirty years earlier, Paul Cain, one of the famous Kansas City Prophets, had prophesied that there would be a revival in London in 1990, which never came to pass. These examples make us wonder:

- What happens when prophets get it wrong?
- Are there consequences for misleading God's people?
- What would a genuine prophet look like today?
- How can you tell a false prophet from a genuine one?

In recent years, misjudgments among charismatic Christians claiming to speak for God as well as moral failures within evangelicalism have resulted in a crisis of belief. In *Prophetic Integrity*, bestselling author and speaker R. T. Kendall gives a warning to those speaking in God's name and offers a way forward in trusting God despite the failures of the church.

Pleasing God: The Greatest Joy and Highest Honor

R. T. Kendall (Foreword by Susie Hawkins)

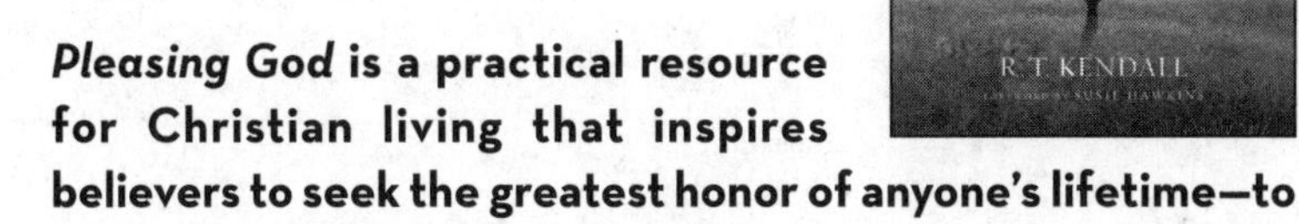

***Pleasing God* is a practical resource for Christian living that inspires believers to seek the greatest honor of anyone's lifetime—to have the privilege of pleasing God.**

Christ's total forgiveness means that we do not have to earn our salvation. When we give our lives to Jesus, we are justified by faith alone. Good works are not required. Prayer is not required. Practicing total forgiveness is not required. Wow—what a gift! But it's likely that if you have been born again, you want to do good works. You want to pray. You want to forgive and love your enemies. Ultimately, you desire to please God.

In *Pleasing God*, bestselling author and well-known preacher R. T. Kendall unfolds the meaning of persistent faith. Starting with the story of Enoch, Dr. Kendall explores biblical teachings that call believers to "find out what pleases the Lord" (Ephesians 5:10 NIV).

With biblical teaching, personal stories, and humble wisdom, Dr. Kendall answers these questions:

- What pleases God (and what displeases him)?
- Why should we please God?
- How should we please God?

Imagine the joy and peace that will come from pleasing God more than seeking approval from others. The world needs this book!